SURVIVAL SKILLS FOR KIDS

How to Perform First Aid, Build Shelter, Start a
Fire, Find Water, Handle Emergencies,
Predict the Weather, and Master the
Wilderness!

Peter Myers

ISBN: 978-1-962496-05-6

For questions, please reach out to Support@OakHarborPress.com

FREE BONUS

^^ SCAN ME!

GET OUR NEXT BOOK FOR FREE!
Scan or go to:
OakHarborPress.com/Free

TABLE OF CONTENTS

INTRODUCTION

What comes to mind when you hear the term "survival skills"? You may instantly think of being lost or stranded somewhere and need to take care of your basic needs, such as shelter, food, and water. While most of us will never find ourselves in such a situation, it's important to develop skills that help you stay safe, feel comfortable in nature, and develop confidence in your ability to solve problems. Survival skills also help you adapt to tough or possibly dangerous situations, and they lay the groundwork for increased self-reliance and resiliency. The younger you are when

1

you gain survival skills, the more well-rounded you will be as you navigate life.

Between the ages of 8 and 12 is the perfect time to not only learn survival skills but also put them to the test. Once you've learned the basics and feel confident, you will stand taller and be able to face challenges head-on. Learning survival skills also provides a sense of responsibility and independence. In addition, you will be proud of yourself and all you've accomplished as you learn and master each task.

In this book, you'll learn how to find water, safely start a fire, navigate with a map and a compass (remember, your smartphone might not work in the wilderness), and watch for changes in the weather that let you know whether you should take cover or continue exploring. These are just a few of the skills you will read about in this book. Along the way, you'll also find activities to try. Some will be easier than others, but they will all allow you to practice what you've learned so far.

When practicing these tasks, especially in the beginning, make sure you have an adult's permission and guidance. Trusted adults will not only give you valuable insight into what you could have done differently but also cheer you on when you're successful. You might even discover a new way to do things all on your own and show the adults a thing or two. It's up to you how little or how much help you accept from them. The good thing is the more you practice, the less help you may need. You might also find that when you answer the call of the wilderness, your family might want to tag along. Hiking and exploring new paths are great ways to spend time with family, especially when everyone is usually doing their own thing. Spending time in nature is also a great way to ease the stresses of the day, week, or school year.

Now that you know what to expect from this book, it's time to get excited about all the cool things you're going to learn. But first, it's important to review a few basic rules.

CHAPTER ONE: BASIC WILDERNESS SAFETY RULES

Before you head for the wilderness, it's important to understand a few basic rules. I know—you probably thought there weren't any rules in the wild, but the rules help keep you, the animals, and the environment safe.

MAKE SURE SOMEONE KNOWS WHERE YOU ARE

One of the first rules to remember is to let a responsible guardian or adult know your plans. Discuss the areas you plan to explore and let others weigh in. You might wonder why you need to do this. Imagine if you and your friends went hiking, didn't tell anyone where you were going, and got lost, or one of you had an emergency. Remember that your cell phones might not work. If the adults in charge don't know where you are headed or what you plan to do, it might take them some time to find you. For everyone's safety, make sure your plans are known.

ALWAYS EXPLORE IN A GROUP

Another crucial safety precaution is to always explore with a group. There is strength in numbers, and when you have friends by your side, you can support and assist one another. Imagine that you and your friends have decided to go camping in a remote location. By staying together, you can better look out for one another, divide up the responsibilities, and help each other problem-solve in an unexpected situation.

DO YOUR RESEARCH

In addition to telling the adults in your life your wilderness plans, it's a good idea to research where you want to go and what you want to do. Researching will help you find out whether there are any rules or regulations in the area you are planning to visit. Also, be sure to check out trail maps, areas you need to avoid, wildlife activity, and potential risks. By doing a little bit of research, you will feel more comfortable when you arrive. Another essential need is to stay on the marked paths. If you stray from the designated trails, you run the risk of getting lost, encountering rocky terrain, and getting injured.

ONLY PACK WHAT YOU NEED

When hiking through undeveloped areas, get in the habit of carrying a backpack for your necessities. You'll soon realize why you should only carry necessities because the longer you carry the backpack, the heavier it will seem. Necessities include water, snacks, a whistle, a flashlight, a compass, and a first aid kit. In addition, make sure you know how to use each of these items and the best practices for a safe adventure. For example, did you know you should have your water bottle filled even when the weather is mild? It's not about needing something cool to drink during the warm months. In fact, even if you don't feel thirsty, you risk becoming dehydrated. The whistle is an important way to alert others to your location in the event of an emergency, and while

7

you might think you'll simply use the flashlight on your phone, having a dedicated flashlight with you on your wilderness trek is a better idea. Additionally, you may need a compass to orient yourself and find your way if you become lost.

DRESS APPROPRIATELY

While you're in the wilderness, you will be around bugs and plants that can cause skin irritation. Along with using sunscreen and insect repellent, you need to dress for the woods. Wear long sleeves and pants that are lightweight, keep you cool, and dry quickly. Additionally, consider a floppy hat to keep the sun off your face and help you cool down during the summer months. On your feet, wear comfortable shoes or hiking boots with textured soles in case the path is slippery. Last but not least, consider packing a poncho, even if the weather forecast doesn't call for rain.

BE RESPECTFUL OF NATURE

It's important to understand the need to preserve natural resources when you're in undeveloped areas. Respecting and protecting the environment is important so that area can stay open to the public and remain safe for both you and the animals living there. You might have heard the saying, "Pack in and pack out." This means to take everything you brought with you when you leave, ensuring the space looks the same after you've passed through. Consider putting a reusable bag in your backpack for your trash. You can also use collapsible containers for any snacks you pack that will take up less space when you're finished with them.

When it comes to interacting with wildlife, it is important to use caution. Hold back rather than approaching them, and do not feed wild animals. Instead, observe their behaviors from afar, take a few pictures, and enjoy the moment. Reacting this way keeps you and the animal safe. Remember, you're in their backyard. Think about how you would feel if someone showed up in your backyard and started poking around!

While animals are interesting and fun to watch, it's important to be aware of the potential dangers linked with certain animals and how to protect yourself from harm. Imagine for a moment that you are walking through the woods, and you come across a snake. Would you know what to do? Do you know which snakes are dangerous to you? Do you know which snakes are common in the area you're exploring? When faced with a snake in your path, back up quietly and give it some space. Most snakes will simply try to escape the situation. They may even be more afraid of you than you are of them. You can protect yourself from potential dangers by understanding what animals you might encounter, their common behaviors, and how to respond when you see them.

It's not only animals that you need to be aware of. Before you head out into the woods, it's important to have a basic knowledge of the local plants, particularly those that are toxic. Some of the most common plants you should immediately recognize are poison ivy, poison oak, and stinging nettles. Identifying them and avoiding them helps you minimize potential reactions. Consider downloading an app for plant identification to help educate you about what plants you might find or, even better, bring a plant guidebook in your backpack in case of cellphone service issues.

WATER SAFETY IS IMPORTANT, TOO

Moving from land to water, the need to pay attention stays the same. You need to understand the potential dangers and observe certain safety recommendations whenever you're around any body of water, whether a river, lake, or pond. For instance, you should know where you can and can't swim. If you're exploring by boat, wear a life jacket that fits you properly, and never swim alone. Do you know how to recognize potentially hazardous currents or underwater obstructions? In addition, diving into unfamiliar waters can cause serious harm. This is especially important because there may be rocks or other hazards lurking just below the surface. Knowing proper water safety techniques can help keep you and your friends safe.

FINAL THOUGHTS

Learning the basic rules and survival skills introduced in this book will allow you to confidently explore the wilderness. By practicing these fundamentals, you can build a solid foundation for responsible participation in outdoor exploration. When heading out on your adventure, travel with like-minded friends and support each other as you explore. These basic rules and survival skills will keep you on the right path for the rest of your life, and the love of nature you develop when you're young will develop in you a lifelong love for nature and exploration.

Activity: Draw or make a list of safety rules to remember when going on a hike or a camping trip. If you're curious about things to add to this list, consider some of the topics discussed above and the categories below.

- Equipment: This list can include the basics you need, like a tent if you're camping, a flashlight, or a compass
- Personal: Don't forget to add sunscreen, insect repellent, or any medications if you have a medical condition
- Food/Water: Extra water and snacks can be listed here, as well as storage bags or containers
- Safety: A first aid kit or rope might go on this list

You can find examples of checklists online for ideas. Once you spend more time in the wilderness, you'll learn what things should be added to your list.

CHAPTER TWO:
FINDING WATER

Before discussing the importance of staying hydrated in the wilderness, let's talk about the benefits of water. Water is a vital component in the maintenance of your health and well-being. Although it may seem unremarkable at first glance, water provides you with several benefits. First, drinking water helps ensure your body is properly hydrated. Because you are nearly 60% water, you have to make sure to drink plenty of it every day to ensure you have enough. When you drink water, you help your body with normal organ, tissue, and cell functioning. Water also helps regulate the temperature of your body, aids in digestion, and transports nutrients. Drinking water also helps you maintain a healthy complexion.

Drinking water daily helps you be the best version of yourself that you can be. You might not realize it, but water is also important for your mental health. When dehydrated, it's hard to focus, access your problem-solving skills, or even make simple decisions. If you want your mind to be as sharp as possible, test how water helps you the next time you have a test or project. Drinking water may give you the extra boost you need to push through and finish studying or complete the last part of the assigned task.

Speaking of boosts, drinking water increases your energy levels. Have you ever felt sleepy or sluggish? You might just need a drink of water to feel revitalized. The circulation of oxygen throughout your body, which gives you essential energy, is facilitated by water. If you want to increase your energy levels naturally, consider sipping a glass of water instead of reaching for a sugary energy drink.

Drinking plenty of water can also help you maintain a healthy weight. When you have a glass of water before a meal, it makes you feel fuller, reducing the likelihood that you will eat an excessive amount of food. Bigger bonus? There are no calories in water. You can maintain your fitness and reduce the calories you consume needlessly if you drink water instead of sugary drinks like soda or juice.

In addition, water is important to your physical well-being. It aids in removing toxins from your body, maintains the health of your immune system, and keeps you from becoming dehydrated. It's the perfect beverage to quench your thirst and keep you feeling good all day.

Now that you know some of the benefits, are you curious about how much water you need a day? The recommended daily water intake for 8- to 12-year-olds is five to six cups. When you're playing sports or exploring the wilderness, you will need more. The best way to make sure you get the water you need is to carry a water bottle with you and refill it often.

IMPORTANCE OF STAYING HYDRATED IN THE WILDERNESS

What does this mean for your adventures in the woods? Well, making sure you have enough water to drink is one of the most important things to consider when you go exploring. As mentioned above, drinking enough water helps you stay mentally and physically healthy, increases your energy level, and helps you with problem-solving and staying focused. Your muscles and joints will also thank you and operate more efficiently, allowing you to easily climb, hike, and navigate the trails. If you start dehydrating, you will feel tired, get muscle cramps, and might not enjoy your time in nature as much as you normally do.

Remember, water helps regulate your body temperature, which is important when you're in the wilderness since the weather might be unpredictable in certain areas. When the weather swings from damp and chilly to humid, your body needs support to manage the change. Water can help. Drinking water also causes you to sweat, acting as a natural cooling mechanism for your body. This action lets your body temperature drop. If you do not drink enough water, however, your body will not be able to adequately cool down. As a result, you may have lightheadedness or even heatstroke, which is a very hazardous condition.

Another hazardous condition might occur if you're not thinking clearly. Since water improves focus, brain function, and concentration, you can imagine why staying hydrated in unknown areas is important, especially since you need to pay attention to keep yourself safe in the wilderness. Dehydration can also affect your ability to concentrate by giving you a headache or causing you to feel unbalanced.

You might think that concentration and focus aren't a big deal. After all, you're in the woods, getting in touch with nature and de-stressing. Do you really need to focus? The answer is yes. Staying alert and focused helps you be aware of your surroundings if the unexpected happens. Maintaining a healthy hydration level while you are out adventuring is important in case something unexpected occurs. Additionally, if you become disoriented or injured, having enough water might keep you alive until assistance arrives.

In summary, make sure you pack enough water to keep hydrated and drink it consistently during your hike, whether you feel thirsty or not. Water keeps your energy levels up, helps you stay cool, enables you to think clearly, keeps you healthy, and prepares you for any unexpected scenarios that might come your way. The next time you look at a glass of water, you might see it differently now that you know all it can do for you. But what happens if you run out of water, and you need to find it while you're in the woods? The next sections will talk about how you can find, collect, and purify water to keep hydrated, focused, and safe.

LOCATING WATER SOURCES IN THE WILD

Finding water in the wilderness might be a lot like a scavenger hunt. Unless there's a well-known path to a pond, you'll have to find clues to get you where you need to be. You might be wondering why this matters. You have your water bottle with you — shouldn't that be all you need? In a perfect world, yes. You would have enough water with you to last the entire day and never have to worry about it, but what if you get lost? What if the temperature climbs higher than you thought it would, or the hills are steeper than you imagined, and you drink your water and your extra bottle halfway through the day? When you start to feel a scratchiness in your throat or find it hard to swallow, you'll be glad you know how to find water in the woods. In fact, finding water in these circumstances can mean the difference between life and death. This next section will give you all the knowledge and skills you need to locate water, assuring your survival in a variety of circumstances. So, what are you waiting for? Let's get started and learn how to find water in the wilderness.

THE IMPORTANCE
OF WATER FOR
SURVIVAL

We talked about the importance of water for your physical and mental well-being above. To recap, remember that water is essential for maintaining temperature, carrying nutrients, and removing waste. Your body is more than half water. Weakness, lightheadedness, and the inability to focus can result from dehydration. This is why finding water becomes much more important in environments where there is limited access to clean, safe water sources. Bottom line? Knowing where to look for and how to collect water in the wild is crucial.

TRYING TO FIND CLUES:
A SCAVENGER HUNT
FOR WATER

Just as you're made of water, nature is made of water as well. Nature frequently leaves us with hints that can direct us to water sources. Our surroundings can provide us with cues that point us in the right direction if we pay close attention to them. The existence of animals and insects is one important indicator. Just like humans, animals require water. When you pay attention to their behaviors or listen to bird calls, you can quickly find probable water sources nearby.

You also gain a lot by paying attention to how the land is shaped. Natural reservoirs are frequently created when water collects in valleys or low-lying regions between hills or mountains. Paying attention to the environment around you can help you find hidden water.

Plants also provide clues to nearby water. Look for thick patches of greenery, especially in drier areas. Cattails, willows, and reeds are examples of plants that commonly grow close to water. As a result, their existence can serve as a trustworthy indicator of the presence of water. Spend some time observing the plants around you and utilize their cues to help you focus your search. Remember that plant app or guidebook? When looking through it, see if there's a section on water-loving plants in the forest and learn to identify those plants.

Speaking of your backpack, you might consider adding a small shovel or trowel to it. You can find collapsible shovels at outdoor adventure stores. If all else fails, you might be able to use a sturdy stick, but it will take longer. Why is this important? Because you can also dig to find water. Finding water can be difficult in dry areas due to the lack of readily apparent sources. There are methods you can do to improve your odds of finding water. One such technique is digging for water. Search for spots with moist soil or close to plant roots because these are more likely to have concealed water. You can locate a much-needed water source by digging a hole and waiting patiently for the water to seep into it.

In the wilderness, rainwater is a precious resource. You have the chance to gather water when it rains, when you come across puddles, or when dew is on the leaves. Remember those collapsible snack containers? You can use them to collect rainwater. If you don't have containers, you can also use fabric or clothing to sponge up the water. You will need to filter the rainwater before drinking it to get rid of any harmful impurities, which will be covered in the next section.

METHODS OF
WATER PURIFICATION

It is essential to clean any water you find in the wild before drinking it to make sure it is safe. One efficient way to get rid of germs and parasites is to boil water over a fire. If you have water purification tablets or drops, purify the water according to the directions on the packaging. Utilizing a portable water filter or purifier to remove contaminants from the water is an additional alternative. These tools are made to get rid of dangerous particles and germs, making the water safe to drink. If you don't have any purifying equipment, you can create a filtration system from materials you find around you, like gravel, charcoal, and sand. Although it might not completely get rid of every impurity, this method is better than nothing. Keep in mind that cleaning your water is necessary to safeguard your health and prevent waterborne diseases. Continue reading to learn more about each method.

Water purification tablets: These can be found online or in stores that focus on survival gear. They're easy to pack and don't take up much space. In general, you can follow these steps when using water purification tablets.

1. Choose the water purification tablet that is right for the type and amount of water you want to clean. There are different brands on the market, so make sure to follow the directions that come with the ones you purchased.

2. Fill a clean jar with the water you want to clean. It's best to start with clear water and filter it through a cloth or fine mesh if needed to get rid of any obvious debris or sediment.

3. Carefully read the instructions that come with the tablets and do what they say. There may be different instructions for different brands and types of tablets, so it's important to follow what the maker says, even if you've used water purification tablets before.

4. Drop the right number of tablets into the water to clean it. How many tablets you need to use will depend on the brand and how much water you want to treat. Most of the time, one or two tablets are enough to treat at least 33 ounces of water, but you should check the directions for exact measures.

5. Dissolve the tablets by slowly stirring the water.

6. Be patient. Each type of water purification tablet has a different contact time, which is how long it needs to be in contact with the water to work. It can be as short as a few minutes or as long as a few hours. When buying your tablets, read the directions to find out how long you need to wait.

7. Leave the water and tablets alone for the time instructed. This lets the tablets kill any germs or microorganisms in the water.

8. After the contact time is over, look at the directions to see if there are any more steps to take. Some tablets may need to be taken with a neutralizing tablet to get rid of any taste or smell left over.

9. Once the water has been cleaned, it should be safe to drink or use for other things. But if you can still see dirt or sediment in the water, you should run it through a clean cloth or a portable water filter before drinking it.

Remember that it's very important to follow the instructions that come with your water purification tablets, as different brands and types will have different steps. Also, keep in mind that water purification tablets mostly get rid of microbial contaminants and might not fully remove some chemical pollutants or heavy metals. If chemicals or toxins have gotten into the water, it may need to be cleaned in a different way.

Boiling water: Have you ever heard someone say that the water in your home is under a "boil order"? This means that somewhere along the line, contaminants have entered the water source, and the water needs to be boiled before drinking it or using it for cooking. You can also boil water in the wilderness to make it safe for you to drink. To use this method of purification, you'll need something to hold the water and fire. The best-case scenario is that you have a lighter or matches to start your fire. If not, there's a section on starting a fire later in this book. You will need to ensure the water is hot enough, which means that there are rolling bubbles, for at least five minutes before taking it off the fire. Then, it's important to wait until it cools completely.

Filtration or purification pumps: These nifty gadgets take the guesswork out of purifying water and don't require you to build a fire. They can be found at stores that sell adventure gear. Essentially, you pour the water that needs to be cleaned into the pump, and drinking water comes out the other end. The system cleanses the water using a charcoal filter. You might also find water bottles that have filters built in, eliminating the need for a separate pump. Remember to carry extra filters with you in case you can't remember the last time you changed it out.

Make an evaporation trap: If you are unable to find water to purify, you can still create a water source using a few basic materials. Building an evaporation trap takes some time, and you'll have to carry a few things with you, but knowing how to make one is invaluable if you plan to spend a lot of time exploring the wilderness. Continue reading to learn how to create your evaporation trap.

Materials:

- Large container

- Small bowl or cup

- Plastic wrap or some other kind of cover

- Rubber band or tape

- Source of heat — this is optional, but it speeds up the drying process

Steps:

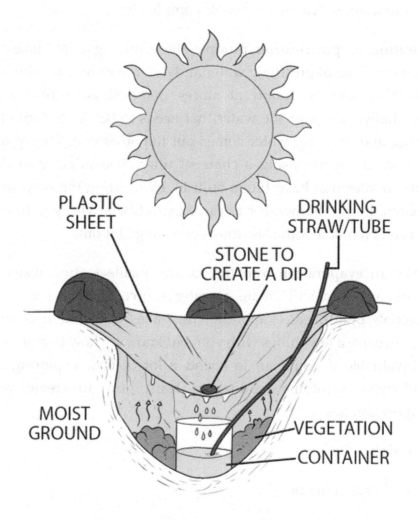

PLASTIC SHEET

DRINKING STRAW/TUBE

STONE TO CREATE A DIP

MOIST GROUND

VEGETATION

CONTAINER

1. Choose a wide, shallow container with a lot of surface area to help the water evaporate. This could be a bowl, a pan, or a jar, for example. If you don't have another container, you can also dig a shallow hole in the ground.

2. Set up a small cup or bowl. This will be the place where the water vapor that has been collected will go. Put it in the middle of your larger container.

3. Put a piece of plastic wrap or something similar over the large container and make sure it covers the opening and the small container fully. Let some of the plastic wrap hang over the sides of the large container.

4. Use a rubber band, rocks, or tape to wrap the sides of the large container with plastic wrap. Make sure it seals well to keep air from getting out.

5. Make a depression over the small container by gently pressing down on the plastic wrap above it with your hand or a small object to make a depression or "dip" right above the cup. A small work will work! This will help guide the water vapor that has collected into the cup.

6. Place the trap in a sunny or warm spot. Evaporation happens more quickly when it is warm, so putting the trap in the sun or near a heat source can speed up the process. The trap will still work without a heat source. It will just take more time.

7. Wait for the water to evaporate. As the water in the big container evaporates, the water vapor will condense on the plastic wrap and collect in the depression above the small container.

8. Check the trap every so often and carefully take out the small container to collect the condensed water. Then you can put it in another jar or use it for whatever you want.

Keep in mind that this evaporation trap works by catching water mist and turning it back into liquid water. It's not a very good way to collect water on a big scale, but it can be useful in some situations. It's a good idea to try this out at home so you know how long it takes and what types of containers to use before needing to do so out in the wilderness.

ADDITIONAL WATER SOURCES

In addition to the methods already stated, there are more potential water sources in the wilderness. Pay attention as you're exploring, and look for any ponds, lakes, or rivers. You will still need to clean this water, but it is more easily accessible than making an evaporation trap. If you've not passed any sources of water, pay attention to the animal tracks you see. These tracks can point you toward water since the animals need water themselves.

It's crucial to use water properly and conserve it as much as you can when you come upon it outdoors. Remember that water is a limited resource and that you might not be able to predict when or where you will next have access to it. Do your best to just sip your water rather than gulping it down, even if you're incredibly thirsty. A little can go a long way. For cooking, cleaning, and personal hygiene, use only a small amount of water. If possible, gather extra water and keep it in containers for later use. Your water supply will last longer if you practice water conservation, improving your chances of surviving in the wild.

Being stranded outdoors without access to a water source can be challenging and dangerous. When tasked with finding water, keep your composure, look around you for hints, and use natural indications like plants and animals. You may need to dig for water, collect rainwater, and purify any water you find; these skills can help keep you alive.

Activity: Practice collecting water by making an evaporation trap or using a filtration system to get the hang of it. The more you practice, the more confident you will be. Follow the steps above to help you create an evaporation trap or the instructions included in your filtration system.

CHAPTER THREE:
SECURING OR BUILDING
A SHELTER

If you plan to camp in the wilderness, securing a reliable place to take cover is crucial for ensuring protection from the elements. It doesn't matter what the weather is like when you leave your home, the natural environment can shift in an instant, and it's best to be prepared. A strong shelter can operate as a barrier, offering protection from severe conditions and serving as a place to relax or sleep. In addition to preventing you from getting wet, keeping you warm, and making you feel comfortable, adequate shelter protects your health and well-being. A good shelter provides a feeling of safety, which helps you reset after a long day of hiking through the woods.

The most obvious shelter for overnight outdoor activities is a tent. Tents are a fantastic investment since they offer protection from the wind, rain, and insects. Below are some tips for purchasing and using a tent.

THINGS TO CONSIDER WHEN BUYING A TENT

When preparing for a hiking trip, investing in a sturdy tent is essential to guarantee a pleasant and safe time spent in the great outdoors. A decent camping tent for trekking should give protection from the elements, be lightweight and portable, and have easy assembly. It's important to consider the tent's size and capacity, resistance to the elements, weight, longevity, ease with which it can be set up, and any special features. Ask an adult with outdoor experience to help you decide when choosing a tent. You can find tents on display at outdoor stores to see what they should look like. You can also read reviews of tents online to learn how easy they are to set up. If you're in the store, take pictures if you choose one that's displayed so that you have a reference when you set it up later.

If you have a tent, follow the directions included. Additionally, it's a good idea to practice building and taking down your tent a few times before ever taking it on an adventure. This way, you'll know how long it will take, how many people you need, and any shortcuts you can take to make assembly faster.

Dimensions and Capacity

Before buying a tent for hiking, you need to think about how many people will be using it. Remember, you shouldn't be in the woods alone, so you can count on at least one other person sharing the tent with you unless you and your companion both have tents. Tents are often labeled with their maximum capacity, such as being able to accommodate one person, two people, or an entire family. It is important to keep in mind that the number of people that a tent is advertised as being able to comfortably accommodate may not always be accurate. Because of this, it is sometimes a good idea to select a tent with a capacity that is one size greater than the number of people who will be using it. In addition, it is important to evaluate the floor area and headroom of the tent to guarantee that there will be enough space inside for sleeping and storing gear.

Your Tent Needs to Be Weather Resistant

Tents designed for hiking adventures should provide dependable protection against a wide range of weather situations. Try to get a tent with a strong rainfly that reaches all the way to the ground and offers sufficient coverage. During rainstorms, you will remain dry if you have a rainfly that has a high waterproof rating and seams that have been taped. Choose tents that have waterproof flooring as well to help keep water and condensation out. In addition, it is important to consider the tent's ventilation possibilities to avoid a buildup of condensation when the weather is humid.

Consider Weight and Portability

The nice thing about a tent is that you don't have to look around for resources to build a shelter. The bad thing is that you need to carry it with you, and when you're on a hike, every ounce matters. Choose a tent that has a design that finds a balance between its durability and its capacity to be small when packed down. Extremely lightweight tents are preferable for camping since they reduce the total amount of weight that must be carried. Try to find tents built of lightweight materials like Silnylon or Cuben fiber and consider the tent poles' weight. You might also eliminate the requirement to carry additional poles by purchasing a tent that can be erected with trekking poles instead of hauling additional poles.

Choose a Tent Made with Durable Materials

For a tent to survive the demands of hiking and the conditions of the outdoors, durability is absolutely necessary. Look for tents manufactured from durable materials such as ripstop nylon, which can withstand abrasions and tears without damage. Stitching that has been reinforced and strong zippers are additional signs of longevity. In addition, you should consider the tent's ability to endure strong winds and select versions equipped with durable poles and guidelines for additional support.

How Easy Is It to Put Up?

When hiking, having a tent that can be set up quickly and without a lot of fuss is a huge advantage, especially at the end of a long day. Look for tents with user-friendly and uncomplicated setup procedures, ideally, ones that are color-coded or include clip-on components. Tents that stand independently are more convenient than other types since they are simpler to set up and may be moved once pitched. Before your trip, you should get some experience pitching the tent to be more comfortable with the procedure and have a more enjoyable time in the great outdoors.

Other Tent Amenities You Might Consider

Take into consideration the additional amenities that could make your camping trip more enjoyable. Doors in tents equipped with double zippers allow for improved airflow and facilitate simpler entry. Interior pockets help to keep stuff organized and are easily accessible. Built-in shelving or gear lofts provide space for storing footwear and bags, keeping them safe and out of the way of the sleeping area. Additionally, some tents come with footprint additions that may be purchased separately to add a layer of defense to the bottom of the tent.

Picking the best tent for hiking is more important than you might think. With the right purchase, your tent can last for a long time, so take the time to truly learn what you might need. Take these tips into consideration when shopping and ask for guidance.

THINGS TO CONSIDER WHEN BUILDING A SHELTER

Even if you're not quite ready for camping, the truth is that anything can happen, even on a day trip in the wilderness. For example, if you are hiking and take a wrong turn, you might find that you need shelter for the night, so it's best to educate yourself about how to create a shelter. Even if you never need the information, it's good to have it. As you explore the wilderness, knowing how to build shelter will serve as your defense against the unpredictability of the journey and the natural world.

In the event you don't have a tent, don't worry! You can find things in the woods to help you out. Look around for long branches or logs that are solid that you can use as the framework for your shelter. You'll also want to create an insulation layer by using smaller branches, leaves, or even moss to help keep you warm and dry. Remember your plant app or book? Consult it when gathering wood to make sure you aren't reaching for something that has poison oak or poison ivy on it.

When it comes to building a shelter in the wilderness, there are several things to take into consideration that can make a big difference in your level of protection and comfort. First and foremost, location. Try to find a spot that is level, slightly elevated, and far away from any potential dangers, such as being prone to flooding or falling limbs. Once you've found a site that will work for you, it's time to evaluate the resources that are close by. Search the surrounding area for solid rocks, trees, or other natural forms that could form the basis of your shelter or provide it with support. For instance, you might be able to find two solid trees on level ground and build your shelter between them.

Next, give some thought to what you will use to build your shelter.

Before beginning your structure, think about how big or small you want the shelter to be, as well as the design. A smaller shelter is better at retaining your body heat than a larger one. A design that is low to the ground and slanted can help deflect wind and rain, which is key if you're in a wetter area. In addition to this, your roof will need to be strong and waterproof. This will prevent any water from getting inside. You might want to use overlapping branches, bark, or even a tarp. If you've ever watched survival shows, you've probably seen them build shelters. Another key piece of advice is to gather everything you need before you start building. Try to have just a bit more than you need to make sure you don't have to go out looking again.

Another important factor to consider is the ventilation. Condensation can be avoided, and you can prevent the shelter from becoming humid or stuffy if you have good airflow. Build the shelter so there are small areas that allow for air circulation without jeopardizing your level of protection. Finally, you should check the shelter's durability before settling in. Give it a good shake to make sure it can take the pressure of wind and rain. If you notice areas that need more reinforcement, make the needed adjustments before moving on.

Always keep in mind that to construct a shelter in the woods, you will need to be resourceful, adaptable, and creative. Building a shelter takes problem-solving skills and practice. Practice at home, either using the tent you purchased or by gathering natural materials to see how they hold up against the elements. Eventually, you'll be able to build a dependable shelter that gives you the comfort and protection you require when you go adventuring in the wide outdoors.

Building a shelter can be a fun way to bring out your creativity and learn more about the natural resources in your own backyard. You might be surprised by how strong branches can be when woven together or that rocks can provide natural cooling. The more you experiment, the more confident you will be. Don't be afraid to ask for help or get suggestions from an adult. They may have ideas you've not thought about.

A DEEPER LOOK
AT LOCATION

Location was mentioned as the top priority above but not fully explained. Since it's the first step, we need to examine why it's important. When you find yourself in the woods or any other type of wilderness situation, it is impossible to overstate just how important it is to select a suitable area to build your shelter. Your choice of location can greatly impact the level of comfort and safety you enjoy, as well as the overall quality of your time spent outside. In order to find the ideal location for your shelter, consider several essential aspects, such as the surrounding topography, natural resources, and potential dangers.

When looking for an appropriate place, terrain is one of the first factors to be evaluated. You need to look for a level surface or one that slopes gently away from you. This area should be free of rocks, roots, and any other uneven ground that could make sleeping uncomfortable or increase your risk of injury. Stay away from low-lying places due to the potential for a sudden rain shower or even a storm. These areas are more likely to be flooded than higher ground. Additionally, you need to think about how the site will drain. This is why a place that slopes away from you is important, to ensure that water won't pool there or get inside when it rains.

Access to natural resources is another critical factor in your ability to build the best shelter. Look for a location that features a lot of different materials you can use for construction. Using trees as anchors, particularly those with thick trunks and branches that dangle at a low height, can help stabilize a lean-to or tarp shelter. Your building process will be less frustrating and more effective when these resources are nearby. Additionally, consider the possibility that your shelter already contains fallen branches, leaves, or other types of plant material that could be used for insulation, padding, seating, or even as a temporary mattress.

Not only that, but your shelter will be easier to conceal if there are thick shrubs or bushes surrounding it. This will also provide protection from the wind. Just make sure to pay attention to any plants or bushes that might be dangerous, either due to an allergic reaction or their own protective measures, such as thorns. Knowing what's around you that you can use to your benefit as well as what you should avoid, helps you be a better-informed adventurer.

Just as important as finding the right location for your shelter is keeping potential dangers and safety issues in mind. Steer clear of any areas that are near dead or unstable trees since these might present hazards in the form of falling branches during high winds. Also, use caution in areas that are prone to landslides and falling boulders and debris, particularly on slopes and near cliffs. Before heading out into the woods, you should know about the dangers in the area you are exploring.

Also, keep an eye out for signs of wildlife, such as animal tracks, burrows, or nesting sites. These are all possible clues that wildlife is present. Although interactions with certain species of wildlife can be fun and exciting, it is critical to remember not to disrupt their natural environments or trespass on their territory in any way.

Now that we've talked about the physical aspects let's talk about the location itself. Take, for instance, the closeness of the location to available water sources. Putting up your tent or building a shelter near a body of water can make it quick and simple to access that water. As mentioned above, though, beware of the possibility of floods or rising water levels during periods of severe rainfall or melting snow.

In conclusion, selecting the ideal spot in the woods or any other natural setting in which to build your shelter is important for your comfort, safety, and overall enjoyment of the experience. You can choose a location that offers the highest level of protection and the greatest amount of convenience by following a few steps. When you're on the trails, take the time to look around and find spots that might be good for a shelter, even if you aren't camping on that trip. Being aware of what's around you can be vital in an emergency.

Another thing to consider is the movement of the sun during the day when planning where to put your shelter. If it is at all possible, you should place it in a position so the entrance or opening faces east. This will allow you to benefit from the warm sunlight in the morning. Whether building a shelter or not, being mindful of the sun's location helps you know what direction you are headed in and what time it is. See Chapter 6 for more details about how the sun can help you in the wilderness.

Different Types of Shelters

Types of Shelters You Can Build

You might decide to try building a shelter, or, as mentioned above, you might find yourself in a situation where you need shelter unexpectedly while hiking. Earlier, we talked about natural resources you can use to build a shelter, but we didn't explore what types of shelters you could build. The good news is that you have options that range from simple to more complex. Keep reading to learn more about these options and maybe gain a few ideas of your own.

Shelter With a Lean-To

A lean-to shelter is among the simplest and quickest options for a wilderness shelter. Two support posts, a ridgepole, and an angled roof composed of branches, leaves, or a tarp are required for this. The open side of the shelter should be oriented so it is protected from the sun and wind, and the roof should be sloped so that water drains off easily. While providing you protection from the wind and rain, this shelter is also great for air circulation. A lean-to shelter functions well as a temporary shelter during daylight rest stops or when used in conditions of light to moderate rain.

Debris Hut

The debris hut is a tried-and-true method for finding shelter in the wilderness that offers superior insulation and defense against the weather. The process entails constructing a framework out of large branches and covering it with multiple layers of leaves, moss, grass, or any other accessible natural material. It is recommended that the shelter be constructed on a raised platform or a bed of leaves to prevent moisture from the ground from entering the structure. The entry should be positioned to reduce the likelihood of drafts, so it is not exposed to the wind.

When building a debris hut, pay attention to the materials you use. You need your branches to be strong to provide the best protection. This type of shelter is better than a lean-to structure if you are likely to need it for more than a few hours. Also, if you pack a tarp, you can use it for flooring within your structure. A braiding technique for thinner branches might be utilized to provide even more protection on the roof of this hut.

Tarp Shelter

Speaking of tarps—did you know you can use them as a makeshift shelter? The tarp shelter is an alternative that is not only adaptable but also lightweight and enables a quick and easy setup. You only need a large tarp, some paracord or rope, and a few stakes to complete this project. Depending on the circumstances, the tarp takes various shapes, such as an A-frame or a diamond, depending on how it is to be used. The tarp will give you good air circulation and offers excellent protection from the wind and rain. This is sometimes the favorite approach for many hikers on longer hikes, as it is easy to carry. Building an A-frame shelter using a tarp only requires a few steps.

Materials needed:

- Tarp

- Cords or ropes

- Strong sticks or tent pegs

- Trees to hold the tarp in place

- Optional bungee cords or extra ropes for extra support

Steps:

1. Find a spot with two strong trees or vertical supports (like poles) that are the right distance apart. The distance should be just a little bit longer than the tarp.

2. Lay the tarp flat on the ground and fold it crosswise to make a triangle. Make sure the tarp is spread out properly and there are no wrinkles or other things in the way.

3. At each corner of the tarp, fold over a small piece, about one foot, and tie a rope or cord tightly around it. These loops will be used to connect the tarp to the frames that will hold it up.

4. Stand at one end of the tarp and lift it up so that the folded edge is at the top. Attach the corner loops to the trees or supports and pull the tarp tight so that the folded edge forms the A-frame's top. You can tie the ropes to the posts with knots or hitches.

5. Fold over the two remaining corners of the tarp and tie a rope or cord around them. Spread the ropes out and tie them to the ground with tent stakes or strong sticks placed at an angle into the ground. This will help keep the sides of the shelter tight and the structure stable.

6. Check how tight the tarp is and make any necessary changes to the ropes to make sure the structure is stable. If you want to make the shelter even stronger, you can tie the tarp to the ground or to other nearby structures with more ropes or bungee cords.

7. Go inside the shelter and look for loose spots or places that might leak. Make any necessary adjustments to ensure your structure is secure from drafts and leaks as much as possible. Once you're happy with its placement and stability, your tarp-covered A-frame shelter is done.

Remember to think about the weather and pick a good place to build your shelter. A shelter made with a tarp can protect you from light rain and sun, but it might not be good for heavy rain or other extreme weather.

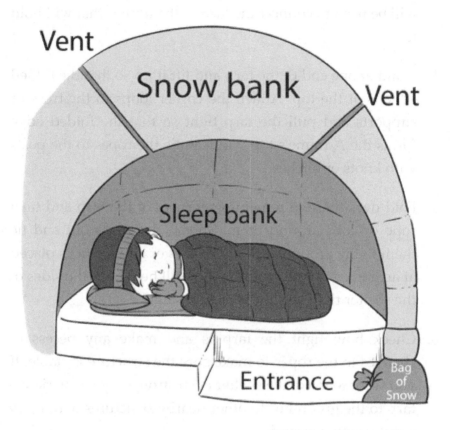

Did someone say extreme weather? You might never need to build a shelter in the snow, but in case you do, it's good to know you can. In fact, in places where there is a lot of snow, a snow cave can be a very useful place to take shelter. Building a snow cave might require you to dig into an existing snowbank or build a snow pile and then hollow out the inside of the pile. The cave's floor, walls, and roof all provide great insulation, which helps to retain body heat and shields you from the cold and the wind. As with all the other shelters, it is essential to have adequate ventilation. Consider a small vent near the entrance to help with this. Constructing a

44

snow cave takes skill and experience, but once it's done, it provides unrivaled protection from the harsh elements of winter.

Tipi or Wigwam Shelter

A wigwam or tipi s a type of shelter that can be built out of wooden poles and big sheets of fabric or tarps. The covering is fastened all the way around the poles, which are arranged in a conical formation. This kind of shelter is sufficient in size, has a strong ventilation system, and is appropriate for prolonged stays in the wild. Due to the increased amount of time and work required to create it, however, it is not recommended if you won't be in one spot for long. The tipi is also more easily constructed when there are larger groups of hikers with you.

When going camping or on other adventures in the woods, having a shelter that you can rely on is necessary for your safety and comfort. Although tents are the most frequent sort of wilderness shelter, experimenting with different types of shelters can give a sense of independence and a connection to the natural world. Every style of shelter, from the most basic lean-tos and debris huts to the most complex wigwams and tipis, has its own benefits and is best utilized in a certain set of circumstances. No matter what option you choose, practicing creating the shelter will help you feel more confident when you must do it for real. Practice also helps you weigh the pros and cons and make the decision that is best for you.

Activity: Look around your backyard and see what items are available to build a shelter. Remember everything you've learned and consult the list below when looking for materials. When you have what you need, decide what type of shelter you want to build and start practicing.

- Branches, logs, and tree trunks can be utilized to build a shelter's general structure.

- Branches with broad leaves can be used to make thatched walls or as a roofing material. You can also braid thin branches using the following technique:

  Find your materials: Look for flexible twigs with leaves, like willow, bamboo, or other pliable branches you can find in your area. Gather enough twigs to cover the area you want your roof to cover.

  Prepare the branches: Take off any extra leaves or side branches from the main branches, leaving only the long, flexible roots. This will make it easy to work with the branches when braiding.

  Set up a structure: Use sturdy poles or twigs to make a basic frame for your shelter's roof. This will be the main support structure. These poles should be firmly planted in the ground or tied together at the top to make a strong roof frame.

  Begin braiding: Start by taking one branch and securing one end of it to the frame. Weave it over and under the frame as you move horizontally along the frame's length.

  Add more branches: Take more branches and repeat the process of weaving by tying them together with the first branch. Make sure the stems are tightly woven together to make a strong roof. As you go, you can add new branches to keep the braid design going.

Cross and secure: When you get to the end of each branch, cross it with the next branch to keep the braiding pattern going. This method of merging helps to make a continuous roof covering that won't leak. Use string, rope, or natural fibers to make sure that the ends of each branch are tightly attached to the framework.

Finishing touches: Trim any branches that stick out past the framework. Once you're done braiding and have the coverage you want, trim any branches that stick out past the framework to make it look better and more streamlined.

Check and strengthen: Carefully check the structure of the braided roof to make sure it is safe and stable. If there are any weak spots or open branches, tie them down tightly to the frame or add more braided branches to help support them.

- Tree bark can be utilized to insulate the shelter or as a waterproof covering.

- Stones and boulders can be used to make a foundation or as wall-building materials.

- Soil and clay can be used to construct walls or a cob building, which is a mixture of earth, sand, and straw.

- Long grass and reeds can be utilized as thatching material for a shelter's roof or walls.

- Moss can be utilized as insulation or as a natural waterproofing material.

- Strong and flexible vines can be utilized to tie or lash the structural components of the shelter together.

- Bamboo is a versatile building material for walls, frameworks, or even entire structures.

CHAPTER FOUR: STARTING A FIRE

Fire is an important part of staying alive in dangerous conditions. Even though it seems like a simple need, it's more important than you might think. Fire can save your life whether you're in the middle of nowhere, in the middle of a natural disaster, or stuck in a remote place. It's also important to respect fire, as it can get out of control and cause damage when you don't remain diligent.

In a survival situation, one of the main things fire does is keep you warm. In harsh settings where temperatures can drop, and hypothermia is a real risk, fire can be used as a heat source to keep you warm and maintain your core temperature at a safe level. It's especially important on cold nights or when it's raining or damp outside, making the risk of losing body heat much higher. The fire's heat keeps you comfortable and helps you conserve your energy. You might wonder how fire does this. The following information will help explain how body temperature can impact your energy.

Your body needs energy to stay warm. The body gets its energy from different places and uses it differently to stay warm. When your body is cold, your nervous system slows down and signals your muscles to also slow down. At the same time, more carbohydrates are used by your body to make lactic acid. This lactic acid and the nervous system's decreased activity prompt your body to do all it can to keep the heat inside.

Your blood flow will slow down. When the temperature drops, blood valves narrow, and blood flow resistance increases. The first thing that happens is that blood flow is cut off to the skin and the body's extremities, such as the fingers, hands, and feet. Because of this, these body parts usually get cold the fastest. Essentially, your body tries to limit the blood flow to decrease the energy it takes to heat it. The better the body is at keeping its core temperature in a safe range, the more heat it can store. Unfortunately, blood pressure goes up when blood flow is restricted, changing how the heart takes in blood. This can change how hard the heart must work; if it's cold, it may have to work harder than usual.

The feeling of cold sets in. To bring its temperature back up, the body will try to heal itself by letting muscles and organs shake inside the body. This is what most people call "shivering." However, this method takes a great deal of energy and isn't very effective. Functioning without heat can lead to major injuries like frostbite and hypothermia.

Without staying warm, your body becomes defensive, and you feel sluggish and in jeopardy of long-term damage. This is just one of the reasons why fire, as a heat source, is essential to survival.

Fire is also an important source of light. When it's dark, fire can help you see better and move around more safely. This light is useful for getting around and doing things like making food or building your shelter. It also helps ease your fear and anxiety by decreasing the darkness around you and giving you a sense of security and control.

Speaking of food, you may need a way to cook food if you're lost in the wilderness. Fire gives you heat, making food safer and easier to digest. When you cook food, the heat kills harmful germs and parasites that might be in it. Heating the food also makes it taste better. In a survival situation where there may not be many tools, being able to cook food over a fire can greatly improve your chances of staying healthy and energized.

In addition to being useful, fire is also a good way to call for help. When you are lost, lighting a fire can help rescuers find you by drawing their attention to your position. The smoke from the fire can be seen from a long way away, making your location clear. You can even add green plants to create a thicker smoke, which increases your chances of being rescued.

Remember when we talked about purifying water? Water is a key element in that process. In the same way, bacteria are killed by cooking food; you can ensure you drink clean water by boiling it first, then waiting for it to cool. Also, the heat from a fire can be used to dry out wet clothes or tools, making you feel more comfortable and lowering the risk of getting too cold. Fire is also essential for protection. Typically when you have a fire going, animals will be less likely to come around since they might be scared away by the sight and sound of crackling flames.

Ultimately, it's impossible to say enough about how important fire is when lost in the woods. Therefore, learning how to start a fire and keep it going is a very important skill for you to have. And although you might think that starting a fire is as simple as lighting a match or rubbing two rocks together, it can be more complicated than that.

TECHNIQUES FOR STARTING A FIRE

Starting a fire with natural, readily available materials is a basic skill that can come in handy in many situations, whether you're lost in the woods or simply camping. Always remember that it's important to put safety first and follow the rules for the area you're exploring. Also, when practicing fire building, recruit an adult to help you out. This will ensure your safety, especially if the fire starts to get out of hand. Below, we'll look at different ways to start a fire using things you can find in nature, including using a hand drill, a bow drill, flint and steel, a magnifying glass, and a fire plow.

Hand Drill

If you read this and you're thinking about the drill in the garage, we're not talking about the same thing. One of the oldest and most effective ways to start a fire is by rubbing two things together, such as rubbing two pieces of wood against each other to make enough heat to start a fire. The hand drill and the bow drill both use friction to make fire.

To use the hand drill method, you need a fireboard and something to use as a spindle. A fireboard is a flat piece of wood, and a spindle can be any stick that is straight and round. Put the spindle on the fireboard and push down on it with your hands on either side of it. Rotate the spindle quickly back and forth between your palms to build heat through friction. The goal is to make enough heat so that the wood dust made by the friction will start to smoke and catch fire. Take your time. This method takes practice and patience.

Bow Drill

The bow drill method is like the hand drill method, but instead of turning the spindle or stick, a bow is used. This makes the process faster and more consistent, but it does require you to find a few more things. To use the bow drill method, you will need a bow, a string, and a plug, in addition to the fireboard and spindle used for the first method. A better description of each is below.

Bow: The bow should be a strong, bendable stick.

String: This can be paracord or any other strong, fibrous material.

Socket: This is a small tool that you hold in your hand and use to push down on the spindle.

Start by wrapping one end of the string around the spindle and tying it to the bow. Put the spindle on the fireboard and the socket on top of the spindle. From there, quickly turn the spindle with the bow. The constant movement creates friction, which heats up the machine and sets the wood dust on fire.

Flint and Steel

If you've ever watched shows like *Survivor*, you know that flint is one of the first things the tribes try to earn. This is because it is one of the more effective ways to start a fire. But did you know that you can find flint in nature? River beds are a great place to start your hunt. Since flint is harder than most rocks, it can stand up to the wear and tear that happens when water washes over it continuously. You can find flint hidden in rock as well. Flint chunks will appear as parts that have turned a different color and have grown with the limestone. Additionally, before you even head out to the woods, you can find flint at building sites or on gravel roads. Flint is usually either black or grey and has a surface that often looks like glass. You can test how sharp it is by safely cutting a glass bottle with it. Now, let's talk about using it to start a fire.

To make fire with flint and steel, you will need a piece of high-carbon steel, called a striker, to hit against the flint. People often use old nail files, coil springs, and rusty yard tools as strikers. The impact of the flint and steel makes sparks that can start a fire in a tinder, which is a bundle of easily flammable things like dry grass, birch bark, or char cloth. For the steel striker to work well, it should have a sharp, curved edge. Hold the steel firmly against the flint with the pointed edge down. Use a quick downward strike on the flint to send sparks to the tinder. It might take a few tries to get enough sparks to start the fire. Once the sparks catch the tinder, slowly blow on the flame to keep it going and help it burn. To make things a bit easier, you can pick up a flint and steel kit at most outdoor supply stores, but now you know what you need in case you don't have a ready-to-use kit.

Magnifying Glass

Another good way to start a fire is to use a magnifying glass or any other curved lens to use the power of sunlight. This method works by focusing the sun's rays on a small spot to make enough heat to start a fire.

First, find a lens with a convex shape, like the bottom of a glass bottle or a magnifying glass. Holding the lens in one hand, stand between the sun and the brush you've collected. Set the lens at an angle so that a small dot of sunlight falls on the pile. Experiment with changing how far away the lens is from the pile until you get a focused spot of light. Use patience and wait for the spark to light the brush. It is important to keep the lens steady so that the heat can be focused as much as possible. The more you move around, the longer it will take to start your fire.

Fire Plow

The fire plow is another friction-based way to start a fire. It uses a flat piece of wood and a thinner, curved stick. Follow these steps to make this method work well:

Choose a piece of wood that is dry and soft. Soft woods like cedar, poplar, or cypress work well because they have a lot of fibers and can easily create friction.

Use a knife or any tool with a sharp edge to cut a long groove along the length of the floor. This groove should be about an inch wide and half an inch deep.

Find a stick with a pointy end that fits into the gap in the baseboard. This stick is called the plow.

Put your brush pile, or tinder, at the end of the groove so the dust from the friction can gather and catch fire.

Put the plow firmly in the groove and move it back and forth quickly with your hands. When the plow rubs against the baseboard, charred wood dust is made, which can be scraped into the tinder pile.

Keep pushing hard back and forth until the charred wood dust starts to burn and sets the pile on fire. Blow softly on the brush to keep the spark going and help it burn.

Remember that you should only ever practice starting fires with natural materials in a controlled and safe setting. Local laws and rules about open fires must be respected and always followed. Also, keep fire safety tools like a fire extinguisher or a bucket of water close by to prevent accidents and put out a fire if necessary.

Learning and mastering these methods can give you the skills and confidence to start a fire with natural materials, even in tough situations.

SAFETY RULES AND REGULATIONS

Speaking of the rules, remember that your responsibility depends on your location, as localities often have their own unique regulations regarding outdoor fire. In addition, there are also typical rules that everyone should follow to ensure your safety, the surrounding environment, and the animals that might be in the wilderness with you.

First, you must find a good place for your fire. Find an open area away from trees, bushes, or dry grass that hang over it. Clear the area around the fire of anything that could catch fire, like leaves or twigs. This makes it less likely that the fire will grow out of control. Making a fire pit can keep the fire even more contained. Dig a small hole and put rocks around it. This helps keep the fire inside the pit and stops it from growing outside its borders.

It's important to use the right materials when choosing a fuel for your fire. Gather dry sticks, twigs, and small leaves to feed your fire. These things are easy to light and burn well. Don't use big logs because they can be hard to handle and could cause the fire to get out of hand. When making a fire in the wilderness, it's important to remember that you should only burn wood and not trash or other things that release chemicals into the air.

Having the right tools is also a very important part of fire safety. If possible, you should have water nearby or even a shovel to quickly put dirt over the fire. If your night in the woods is planned, you might also consider having a small fire extinguisher in your supplies.

Next, never leave a fire alone, and always keep a safe distance from it. Keep a close eye on any sparks or flames that might fly out of the fire pit, as they could start a bigger fire. When it's time to put out the fire, let it burn down on its own until all that's left is a bed of hot coals. If you have water, you can use it to speed up the process. Additionally, move the ashes around and ensure no coals or hot spots are left. It's important to be thorough because a fire that seems to be out can start up again if it's not put out properly. If you take your time and follow the proper steps, you can ensure the fire is out before you leave the area.

Even if you only plan to be in the woods for the day, take the time to pay attention to all the rules while you're there, not just the ones that seem pertinent to you. After all, you might find yourself lost or out later than you thought you might be. The first rule of safety is to be prepared. Information about rules and regulations for your location can often be found online or at Welcome Center or ranger station if you're in a park.

Activity: Create your own flint and practice making a fire.

Even though it may not work as well as store-bought flint, using an old nail file to make flint can be useful, especially in an emergency when there aren't many ways to start a fire. Here are the steps to use an old nail file to make your own flint:

Gather the things you need. To make your own flint, you will need an old nail file or any other piece of hardened metal that can be hit and make sparks. You will also need something to hit the flint with, like a hard rock or another piece of metal, to test what you've made.

Get the nail file ready. Take a close look at the old nail tool. Look for the side of the file that is rough and coarse. This is the side that will make sparks. You can use a file or sandpaper to make the surface even rougher if you need to. The goal is to make a rough, bumpy surface to make sparks when it is hit.

Find a good place to strike the flint. Look for a hard, strong surface that you can hit the flint against. This can be a flat rock, a piece of metal, or even the back of your knife. Make sure the surface you hit is stable and won't break if you hit it repeatedly.

Gather your fire-starting materials. Before making sparks to test your flint, get your fire-starting materials together. Make sure the things you use to start a fire are dry and easy to light. This can be dry tinder like small twigs, dry leaves, cotton balls, or bigger fuel like small trees or logs. You also want to make sure you're in an area where you're allowed to start a fire and that it is safe to do so. Ask an adult to help you with this activity to ensure your safety.

Strike the flint: Hold the nail file tightly between your thumb and index finger, with the rough side facing the flint. Set the file at a small angle and hit it hard against the surface you're using. Aim for a sharp, glancing hit to the file to increase the chances of sparks. You might have to hit the flint more than once before a spark starts to fly.

Direct the sparks: When hitting the flint, aim the sparks toward your prepared fire-starting material. Set up the fire so that it can easily catch the sparks. The idea is to get the sparks to land on the brush or tinder so that it can catch fire.

Ignite the fire: Once you've made sparks and gotten them to land on the tinder, blow gently on the glowing ember to help it grow. Add more wood to the fire gradually, starting with smaller pieces and moving to bigger ones.

Remember that practice is the best way to learn how to use homemade flint to make sparks. It might take time and practice to get good at the skill and make sparks every time. Also, be careful when hitting the flint to avoid hurting yourself.

CHAPTER FIVE: FINDING FOOD

Even if you consider yourself an experienced explorer or adventurer, getting lost in the wilderness is a scary and intimidating experience. Bad weather, unpredictable conditions, and lack of tools worsen this problem. How you handle being lost and how much you've prepared for the worst-case scenario can also affect the situation. If you panic, your mood will plunge, and you'll lose valuable energy. Plus, once you've allowed yourself to fall into a rabbit hole of "what ifs," it's hard to bounce back immediately. Having a game plan for if the inevitable happens is essential. With that in mind, one of the first things you'll need to do is figure out how to find food.

Think of the body as a complicated machine, like a car, in many ways. A car needs fuel to move from one place to another and do what it was made to do. In the same way, our bodies need fuel in the form of food. This fuel helps our bodies work well and gives us the energy we need to complete tasks. Just as a car without gas would stop and be unable to reach its destination, a person who doesn't eat will slowly lose strength, making it harder and harder to keep going.

Your body must work harder to keep up when you're out in the wild. Moving through thick vegetation and rough terrain and even building a shelter all take a lot of physical and mental effort. In a survival situation, you may also need to devise ways to call for help, which again takes energy and a sharp mind. What does this have to do with food? Well, if you don't eat enough, you could get tired and hungry, making you slower and weaker than normal. Needing food also decreases your ability to focus. This deterioration can make it harder for you to make important choices, hurt your physical skills, and lower your chances of survival in the long run.

Consider how your body reacts when you're studying for a big test. As you go through the notes for class, you may feel your muscles tightening, which uses energy. The thoughts that go through your mind, ranging from getting in trouble for a bad grade to having to take the class all over again, cause your stomach to tighten and your head to hurt. You might think that getting lost in the wilderness and learning are worlds apart, but when you break them down, you might realize they're not that different after all. The food you consume while studying can significantly impact your ability to turn things around, refocus, or even stay up later to finish the task. The typical response is to reach for something quick, greasy, and satisfying—also known as comfort food. And while this will sustain you, there might be better choices. Now, let's go back to being lost in the wilderness. Can you see how your body is reacting similarly?

In short, the next time you're studying or packing for your next adventure, focus on adding foods that increase your energy and ability to focus. This way, if you run out of food or need to study one more chapter, you've already been doing your best to keep the body ready to go. Essentially, you're starting with a good foundation, not one built on gummy bears and cold pizza. What are some worthy foods to consider? It's best to focus on foods that give you essential nutrients and energy, are portable, and don't weigh down your stomach or backpack. Some great choices for studying and hiking include the following:

Trail mix. Trail mix is a mix of nuts, dried fruits, and seeds that give you a good balance of protein, healthy fats, and carbs to keep you going for a long time. Several mixes can be found in stores, or make your own from the recipe below.

Ingredients:

- 1 cup of nuts (such as almonds, cashews, peanuts, or walnuts)
- 1 cup of dried fruit (such as raisins, cranberries, apricots, or banana chips)
- 1 cup of whole-grain cereal (such as granola, toasted oats, or puffed rice)
- 1/2 cup of seeds (such as pumpkin seeds or sunflower seeds)
- 1/2 cup of chocolate chips or small chocolate candies (optional)
- 1/4 teaspoon of salt (optional)

Instructions:

1. In a mixing bowl, combine the nuts, dried fruit, whole grain cereal, seeds, and chocolate chips (if using). Mix well to distribute the ingredients evenly.
2. If desired, sprinkle the salt over the mixture and give it another gentle stir.
3. Transfer the trail mix to an airtight container or individual snack bags for storage.

That's it! You can customize this trail mix recipe by adding or substituting ingredients according to your preferences. Feel free to experiment with different nuts, dried fruits, or other tasty additions like coconut flakes or pretzel pieces. Enjoy your homemade trail mix as a convenient and delicious snack on the go.

Energy bars. Choose energy bars higher in calories, protein, and fiber but not too much extra sugar. Look for choices made with whole grains, nuts, and dried fruits.

Jerky. Jerky is the food of champions. Not really, but you don't have to look hard to find people who swear that jerky is the cure-all for everything. No matter which kind you choose, jerky is easy to carry and high in protein, making it a great snack to keep you full. Like trail mix, you can make your own jerky.

Dehydrated meals. These meals are easy to carry, and you only need hot water to eat them. Look for meals with the right amount of carbs, protein, and fat.

Instant oatmeal. Not only is oatmeal a filling breakfast food that is quick and easy to make, but it's also full of energy-producing nutrients. You can choose individual packs or fill resealable bags with the desired amount. You can also opt for snack bars that are oatmeal based to conserve your water.

Nut butter. Peanut and almond butter come in single-serve packets full of healthy fats and can be eaten with crackers, bread, or veggies.

Crackers or rice cakes. These are easy to carry and give you energy by giving you carbs. Look for foods with whole grains to get more fiber.

Dried fruits. Choose dried fruits like raisins, figs, or mangoes, which are full of vitamins and minerals and have natural sugars for energy.

Cheese. Hard cheeses like cheddar or gouda can last the trip and give you protein and fat. You can cut them into smaller pieces that are easier to eat.

Now that you know some foods to consider when packing for your trip, let's look more at the nutrients in the foods and why that's important.

Proteins, for example, are essential for repairing body tissues and boosting your immune system, which helps you fight off infections. This is key if you are hurt or prone to illness and are lost in the woods. On the other hand, fats are also important, even though they sometimes get a bad rap. You need fats to keep heat in your body and help you stay warm.

Also, the vitamins and minerals you get from food help your body do many different things. These nutrients are essential because they keep your defense system, your nerves, and your metabolism working well. Ensuring you are getting enough of these nutrients makes the body much more resistant to the stresses it would face in an outdoor survival situation.

Another often-overlooked reason food is vital in survival is how it makes you feel. Finding and eating food in these situations can boost your mood and helps you feel like you have a sense of control over the situation. This mental boost can help you deal with the stress, fear, and confusion of getting lost in the wilderness. It also gives you hope and drive, which are intangible but essential parts of staying alive.

It's easy to see that finding food when lost in the woods is more than just a way to stop feeling hungry. It's about ensuring you have enough energy and nutrition to face and overcome the many obstacles you may face in the wilderness. It's about improving physical health, mental agility, and emotional strength, all of which are important for life.

Thinking of new ways to get food is also a critical skill in survival situations. In the wilderness, you might not be able to find familiar foods. In fact, you might have to eat things you would never eat in a typical situation. Because of this, knowing the local plants and animals, which plants are safe to eat, how to catch or draw small game, and even how to fish can help you stay alive.

TECHNIQUES FOR IDENTIFYING EDIBLE PLANTS AND FRUITS

Learning how to find food that you can eat in the woods can be fun and valuable. Whether you like nature, want to learn how to forage, or be more self-sufficient, identifying edible plants can help you feel more connected to the natural world and give you a sense of independence, and, of course, it's a valuable skill if you ever get lost. Here are a few things you can do to help you with this.

First, learning about the local plants and what you can and can't eat is vital. Each area has its own plants, some of which may be safe to eat while others may be poisonous or dangerous. Field guides, books, and online tools about your area can tell you a lot about the native plant species and whether they are edible. Remember the app you downloaded earlier? Start by learning about common plants you can eat and what makes them unique.

One helpful thing to do is study the things that make plants easy to identify. Plants have different physical characteristics that can help you tell them apart. Pay attention to the shape, color, and arrangement of the leaves, as these can change a lot from plant to plant. For example, the leaves of some edible plants are shaped like hearts, while the leaves of others may have sharp edges or interesting designs. By learning about these traits, you can spot plant families and make better decisions about whether or not they are safe to eat. It's important to remember that even if a plant's fruit is safe, other parts of the plant, like its leaves or roots, could be poisonous. Before deciding whether the whole plant is safe, you should know more about it.

When studying the plants, take note of anything that stands out, like thorns, hairs, or marks. Some plants have hairy stems or leaves, while others have brightly colored berries or designs that can be used to tell if they are safe to eat. If you pay attention to these things, you'll be able to remember the plants easily and make better decisions.

Look around your area and see if there is a local foraging group. These experienced foragers can teach you about the plants that grow in your area, give you valuable tips and tricks, and help you learn how to identify plants. You can also ask an adult about attending guided hikes or classes to help you get hands-on experience and learn from the practical knowledge of others. It is important to be careful and follow safety rules when looking for food plants. Never eat a plant without knowing for sure what it is first. Even though some plants look like they could be eaten, they might be poisonous or have dangerous look-alikes.

Equally important is to remember that some plants may need to be prepared in a certain way to get rid of poisons or improve their taste. For instance, stinging nettles have hairs that can hurt you if you eat them raw, but they can be quite beneficial for you. To gain the benefits, you need to cook or boil them. As mentioned earlier, some plants have parts you can eat and parts you can't, like rhubarb, where you can only eat the stalks and not the leaves. Because of this, it is crucial to learn the correct way to prepare each plant you want to eat.

Lastly, don't hurt the earth or pick wild plants carelessly. When foraging, take only a little from one place. This will let plants grow back and feed other animals in the environment. Be aware of local laws or rules that say you can't forage in certain places, like on private or protected land. Also, when gathering food plants, be careful not to hurt the plant or the surrounding area.

Identifying food that you can eat in the woods takes time and practice. Always put safety first, keep learning, and give yourself time. With experience and knowledge, you can confidently explore the outdoors and keep your cool if you've taken a wrong turn and are lost.

HUNTING AND TRAPPING ANIMALS

Beyond plants, it might also be essential to understand what animals you can eat in the woods. Learning how to hunt and trap animals in the wild can be useful, especially if you find yourself lost and in need of food. You need to be as safe as possible when doing any of these tasks. In fact, let's start there. The following is a list of critical safety advice that should be kept in mind if you need to hunt or trap animals in the wilderness.

Educate yourself: Gain an understanding of the species of animals that can be found in the area as well as their habits. With this information, you will better comprehend their behaviors, preferred environments, and potential risks. It might be a good idea to take a hunter education class or find experienced mentors who can aid you in learning about animal behavior, tracking techniques, and safe hunting procedures.

Be prepared: Always have a trustworthy knife in good shape for cutting and skinning wildlife. Make sure that it is kept in a secure location to prevent any mishaps.

Use caution: When working with snares, traps, or firearms, exercise extreme caution. If you're not paying attention, you might injure yourself.

Be aware: Always be aware of your surroundings and keep an eye out for any potential hazards or wildlife that could pose a threat to you. Maintain a safe distance from animals. Unless necessary, do not approach them.

Be respectful: Make sure you are hunting and trapping ethically. You should show proper courtesy to any wildlife you encounter and use the resources responsibly. This means you need to refrain from overhunting or catching more animals than you need. This ensures the continued existence of wildlife and assists in the upkeep of a healthy ecosystem.

Firearm safety: If you have access to a gun, follow the safety rules. Always handle firearms as though loaded and ensure that the muzzle is always pointed in a secure direction. Check that your firearm is functioning properly and maintained correctly. Keep each type of ammo in its own secure location. Never point a firearm toward something you don't plan to shoot, and always be aware of your target and the area around it to avoid accidentally injuring someone else.

Employ the appropriate trapping methods: If you plan to use the trapping methods outlined below, you need to make sure that you adhere to ethical trapping practices and use caution when setting them. It is best to avoid utilizing traps that could cause needless pain and suffering. Check your traps regularly to reduce the time an animal is forced to spend in an uncomfortable situation. Unintentional catches should be released as quickly and carefully as possible.

Be smart: Pay attention to your surroundings and make safe decisions. This can be hard, especially when you're scared. Force yourself to slow down and remember the things you've practiced to give yourself the best chance at being rescued.

Now that you understand some of the basic rules, we can look at how you can go about hunting and trapping if you get lost and need food.

Fishing

Fishing is a great option, particularly near bodies of water such as rivers, streams, or lakes. Unfortunately, you might not have a fishing pole with you. That's okay. You can easily make one with the things you find in nature and a few things you pack in your backpack — like a fishing line and a hook. For the pole, all you need is a solid stick. Once you've created your pole, find a good area along the water's shoreline. When you're ready, find a worm or insect for bait. After catching a fish, it is necessary to thoroughly clean and prepare it.

Cleaning the Fish

1. Find somewhere flat and clean to work.
2. Hold the fish tightly and remove the scales with a small knife or scaler. Use short, smooth strokes to scrape from the tail to the head.
3. Make a shallow cut all the way along the side to pull out the insides of the fish.
4. Rinse the fish well with clean water, removing all blood and dirt.
5. You can also remove the head, fins, and tail if you want.

Getting the fire ready to cook the fish — remember the fire tips you learned earlier!

1. Let the fire burn until a bed of hot coals has formed. This will make the cooking temperature more stable.
2. Put the fish right on the hot coals.
3. Depending on the fish's thickness, cook it for about 5 to 10 minutes on each side. Cooking times can be different, so watch it closely.
4. If you have utensils, put a fork or knife into the biggest part of the fish to see if it's done. If the meat is opaque and comes off easily, it's ready to eat.
5. Take the fish carefully off the fire and let it cool down before serving.

Snare Traps

Snare traps are one of the most basic and effective trapping methods. When you set out into the woods, keep an eye out for indicators of animal activity, such as trails or tracks left behind by the game. This way, you not only know what types of animals you might find if you get lost, but you'll also know where to set the traps. To make a snare, build a loop out of a sturdy but flexible wire or cord. The loop should be able to tighten when an animal steps into it. Make certain that the loop is firmly attached to a tree or a stake before proceeding. Put something in the snare that will entice the animal you want to catch, such as some berries or nuts. Place a couple of traps, if possible, and check on them regularly. Also, it is important to release any inadvertent catches to prevent causing any harm to endangered or protected animals.

Pitfall Traps

Pitfall traps are a type of trap that is particularly useful for trapping smaller animals. To set up a pitfall trap, simply dig a deep hole in the ground and then cover it with bushes or sticks to make it appear like it is not there. Put some food or bait at the bottom of the pit so the animal will be enticed to enter. When an animal approaches the bait to eat it, the trap causes it to fall into the hole.

Bow and Arrow

Using a bow and arrow is a form of hunting that has the potential to be successful, but it requires a certain level of skill and practice. Since you most likely won't have the typical bow and arrow with you, consider the following steps to make one with natural materials. It's a good idea to practice this at home in case you truly need it.

Find the materials you need: For the bow, look for a strong, flexible branch or small tree that is about your height or a little bit higher. It should be made of hardwood like oak, hickory, or yew, if possible. Find another straight, light branch or stick to use as the arrow.

Shape the bow: Cut off any smaller branches or twigs and carefully make the bow into a curve with a knife or a sharp rock. When the string is connected, the tension will come from the curve.

Find something strong and flexible to use as the bowstring: You can use paracord, strong plants, or even strips of clothes. Make a notch on each end of the bow and firmly attach the string, making sure it is tight but not too tight. To make the string tighter, you can twist it several times.

Make the arrow: To make the arrow, choose a thin, straight branch or stick for the tip. Knots or side branches should be cut off. Make a small notch on one end of the arrow to hold the bowstring. At the other end, carve a point or attach a sharpened tip of bone, stone, or any other sharp object you can find.

Test and tweak:

1. Carefully test your bow by pulling the arrow back and letting it go.
2. Pay close attention to how stable, fast, and accurate it is.
3. If you need to, make changes to the bow or arrow to improve it.

While it's true that hunting and trapping are useful skills to have if you find yourself in a position where you need to survive, it's important to remember that you should only engage in these activities as a last choice. When faced with any kind of survival scenario, you must put your health and safety first. Suppose you become disoriented when traveling in the wilderness. In that case, it is critical that you maintain your composure, limit your use of physical effort, and look for assistance as quickly as possible. If you go hiking or camping, you should always let someone know your plans, including when you plan on leaving and returning, so they can contact the authorities if you don't come back when you were supposed to.

Remember that having good survival abilities is crucial, but being preventative and well-prepared is much more so. Before going on any outdoor excursion, you should ensure that you are well-prepared in terms of your knowledge, gear, and supplies so that you may safely explore and enjoy the environment.

Activity: Go on a nature walk and identify at least three edible plants or fruits.

When you're lost in the woods, it can be important to know how to find plants with food that you can eat. Here are some general rules to help you figure out which plants are edible:

Prioritize known plants. If you know of any familiar plants or fruits that are safe to eat, look for those first.

Pay attention to the animals. Animals often eat fruits and berries that people can eat, so keep an eye out for birds, mice, and other animals eating plant matter. Be careful, though, because not all fruits that animals eat are good for people to eat.

Study the local plants: Learn about the plants and foods that grow in the area where you are lost. Find out which popular plants you can eat and which you should avoid. Local field guides, apps that help you identify plants, and survival instructions for the area can all be helpful.

Look for signs that the fruit is edible: There are a few ways to tell if a plant is likely to produce fruits that you can eat. Look for plants that look healthy and full of life and show no signs of illness or pests. Pay attention to anything that stands out, like a fruit's shape or color that matches a known edible variety.

Do a thorough evaluation: Before eating any plant, do a thorough evaluation to ensure it is safe to eat. Don't forget the saying, "When in doubt, do without." It's better to be safe than sorry to avoid possible problems.

Do a taste test: If you are sure that you have found a plant you can eat, take a small piece, and rub it on your skin or lips. Wait a few hours to see if there are any bad effects. If nothing bad happens, take a small bite, and wait a long time to make sure you don't have an allergic reaction or adverse effects.

Determining what a plant is can be hard, and getting it wrong can have bad results. It is important to put safety first and not eat a plant unless you are sure it is safe.

CHAPTER SIX: NAVIGATION

We've talked a lot about getting lost, but have you wondered how to stay on the right path in the first place? What do explorers normally use to help them avoid getting lost? Your answer is probably their phone, but remember that phones haven't always been around, and you won't always have service in the wilderness. Not only that, but if you get lost, you may run out of battery on your phone. Before heading out to the woods, it's vital that you learn how to use a compass and read a map. Keep reading to find out more.

Understanding Maps

Maps show us the locations of various items. For every map, there are certain things you'll always find. Knowing how to read these is essential to reading the map.

Symbols indicate various aspects of a map, including the roads, buildings, rivers, and mountains depicted on the map. These icons give us a better understanding of what we are looking at on the map.

The term "scale" refers to a feature on maps that illustrates the proportional relationship between the distances depicted on the map and the actual distances that exist in the real world. For instance, if the scale is 1:10,000, this indicates that 1 centimeter on the map corresponds to 10,000 centimeters (or 100 meters) on the ground.

Maps typically include something called a legend, also sometimes called a key, explaining what the various symbols on the map represent.

Understanding a Compass

Now that you have a basic comprehension of maps, let's move on to compasses and become familiar with their operation:

Compasses have a needle that is oriented in a direction that points towards the magnetic North of the Earth. A compass has a revolving dial that you may turn to determine your direction and a base with degrees inscribed.

As mentioned, the needle of the compass points to the magnetic North, which is somewhat different from the true North or the North Pole. Magnetic North is indicated by the direction that the needle points.

To use a compass to find a direction, hold it flat in your palm so that it is parallel to the ground. Make the necessary adjustments to get the needle to align with the "N" on the dial. The direction arrow at the bottom of the compass currently points in a northerly direction. Take advantage of this information to get your bearings on the map.

To ensure that the map accurately depicts the surrounding environment, set the compass on top of the map in such a way that the base's outer edge points in the desired direction. Together, rotate the map and the compass until the needle on the compass points toward the North.

Putting It All Together

Now that you understand how to read a map and use a compass let's look at how the two tools interact with one another.

Determine your location: Look on the map for familiar landmarks or features in the area immediately surrounding you. Using the compass, you can find out in which direction these features are located relative to your current position. Note where you are on the map by using these recognizable landmarks.

Determine where you want to go: Once you know this, draw a route for yourself on the map based on that decision. Make sure you have the compass with you to figure out which way you need to go. Be sure to consider any potential barriers, such as rivers or mountains.

Keep an eye on the compass and map: Always ensure you're moving in the right direction by checking your map and compass regularly. Keep an eye out for recognizable landmarks along the way so you can track your progress.

Learn About Waypoints

Waypoints are specific places in the world that are used to mark important spots along a route. Most of the time, they are shown by coordinates, like latitude and longitude or locations. Waypoints are like landmarks that help you get from one place to another.

If you're lost in the woods and have planned your route ahead of time or are using a GPS device or a guidance app on your phone, knowing about waypoints can help you find your way. Here's how waypoints can help you find your way when you're lost:

Pre-planned waypoints: If you planned your route before you went into the woods, you might have picked out certain waypoints along the way. These could be landmarks, intersections, or natural features like rivers or hills that stand out. You can try to find these marks on your map or GPS to figure out where you are and how to get where you want to go.

GPS devices and navigation apps: You can put specific waypoints into a GPS device or a smartphone with a navigation app. By following the routes and distances given, you can find your way to the next waypoint and then get to where you want to go.

Natural waypoints: If you don't have any planned waypoints or electronic navigation tools, you can look for natural waypoints in the surroundings. These could be things like unique rock formations, the way trees are arranged, or well-known sites that can help you figure out where you are and find your way. For example, a mountaintop or a river could be used as a landmark to help you find your way to a known place or a nearby trail.

It's important to remember that waypoints alone may not always be enough, especially if you're in a place you don't know or on difficult ground. To make sure you stay safe in the wilderness, it's a good idea to know how to read a map, use a compass, and know some basic survival methods. Always keep in mind that practice makes perfect. Anytime you can grab a map, step outside, and practice finding your way around. The more familiar you are with the map and compass, the more confident you will be when you're in the woods.

TECHNIQUES FOR NAVIGATING WITHOUT A MAP OR COMPASS

When heading into the woods, you should always have at least a compass with you and a map when possible. But things happen, and you might find yourself lost without either item. If this happens, remember to stay calm. Luckily there are ways for orienteering and determining directions that do not involve the use of these maps or a compass.

Making Use of the Sun

Have you ever paid attention to the sun's movements before? Or did you just read that it can help you tell time and your location, and now you're curious if that's true? It is true. The sun has been helping people for centuries. Two ways it can help you while you're in the woods are outlined below.

Using the sun and a stick: Put a stick or other item in the ground vertically so that it casts a shadow. Make a mark on the ground where the tip of the shadow is. Wait about 15 to 30 minutes, then mark the new end of the shadow. Connect the two dots with a straight line. This line is about an east-west line, with the first mark showing where the west is and the second mark showing where the east is. The north-south line goes through the middle of the two marks.

Using the sun to find your way: In the northern hemisphere, you can use a clock face to figure out the general direction of the north. Halfway between the hour hand and 12 o'clock on a horizontal watch with the hour hand aligned with the sun will be south. North is on the opposite side. Use the same technique in the southern hemisphere but align the sun with the position at 12 o'clock.

Finding east and west: The sun rises in the east in the morning. If you face the rising sun, you will be facing east. In the evening, the sun goes down in the west. If you face the sun as it goes down, you will be facing west.

It's important to remember that these methods only give you a rough idea of where to go and how long it will take. They can be changed by things like the season, latitude, and weather in the area. Specialized tools like a sundial or a compass will give you more accurate readings.

Using Natural Signs

What do you do if it's a cloudy day or if the sun is hard to detect in the woods? You're in luck—nature gives us a variety of hints that can guide us in the right direction.

Moss on trees: Moss tends to grow more on the north side of tree trunks in many different places since this side of the tree receives less sunshine. You can use the presence of moss on trees as a general indicator of the direction north by looking for it.

Pay attention to the wind: Find the direction that the wind is blowing from by paying attention to the grass and trees. This can provide you with a general sense of where north and south are located if you're familiar with the general areas since wind patterns tend to be the same.

Finding Your Way Using Landmarks

Landmarks are distinguishable characteristics in the environment that might assist one in navigating their surroundings.

Mountains and hills: Both mountains and hills are prominent features that can be seen from afar and are helpful for establishing a sense of direction. You can utilize a specific peak or hill as a reference point if you are familiar with its general direction and have this knowledge.

Rivers and streams: The water in bodies of water such as rivers and streams often go in one direction rather than another. If you come across one, you should move downstream with it because, most of the time, it will bring you to larger bodies of water and typically more people.

Utilizing the Stars

People have used constellations to find their way for hundreds of years. By looking at and recognizing certain constellations, you can figure out your direction and estimated location. This can help you find your way back or get to a place you know. Even though there are many constellations that can be seen at night, some are better known and can be used to find your way. Let's look at a few of these popular constellations and how they can help you if you get lost in the woods.

The Big Dipper (Ursa Major): The Big Dipper is one of the most recognized constellations in the northern hemisphere. It looks like a spoon and is made up of seven bright stars. Two stars at the end of the spoon point to Polaris, the North Star, which is a reliable way to find your way. By finding the Big Dipper and Polaris, you can figure out where you are in relation to the North.

Orion: Orion is another well-known constellation that can be seen in the northern hemisphere winter sky. It has several bright stars, such as the three stars that make up Orion's belt. If you draw a line through the belt, it will lead you to two bright stars: Betelgeuse and Rigel. These stars can help you figure out which way is east and which way is west. By using Orion, you can figure out which way to go and then get there.

Cassiopeia: Cassiopeia is a unique constellation that looks like a "W" or a "M" based on how you look at it. In the northern hemisphere, you can see it all year long. The location of Cassiopeia in relation to Polaris, the North Star, can help you find your way. If you imagine a line from Polaris to Cassiopeia and follow it, you will end up going north.

Crux (Southern Cross): The star Crux is easy to see in the southern hemisphere and helps people there find their way. It is made up of four bright stars that look like a cross. You can find the south by making a line between the two stars at the long end of the cross. The Southern Cross is especially helpful for finding your way around in the southern hemisphere, where it is low in the sky.

These are just a few examples of popular constellations that can help you find your way if you get lost in the woods. It's important to remember that celestial navigation needs a good view of the night sky without trees or buildings in the way. Also, the position of a constellation can change based on the time of year and where you are on Earth. Before going on any outdoor activities, it's a good idea to learn about the night sky and the constellations that are important to your area.

REMAIN ON THE TRAIL OR PATH

While it's fun to explore, unless you're very familiar with the area, the best thing to do is stay on a dedicated trail or path for various reasons, the most obvious being that you're less likely to get lost if you stay on the path. That being said, things happen, and when they do, you'll need to be prepared. Below, we'll talk about why you should stay on the path and other tips and tricks.

Easy navigation: All the trails and walkways are clearly signposted so that you can make your way through familiar and secure pathways. Especially in places that are foreign to you, straying off the track can result in getting lost.

The path provides safety: Trails are constructed in such a way as to steer hikers away from potential dangers. Maintaining your position on the route lessens the chances of running into these hazards.

Safeguarding the environment: Trails aren't just for your safety. They're also for the safety of the ecosystem and the animals living in the woods. Stepping off the designated path might cause harm to the surrounding vegetation and contribute to soil erosion. Erosion of soil can be detrimental to delicate ecosystems, disruptive to habitats, and off-kilter with the natural order of things. Additionally, wandering off the track has the potential to disrupt the natural behavior of wildlife and the environments in which they live. Keeping to the approved path reduces the amount of human interference and contributes to the conservation of the natural environment for the benefit of both plants and animals.

Staying on the trail or path that you are exploring is not only about following the regulations but also about safeguarding yourself and the environment. When you go on your next adventure, keep in mind how important it is to always keep track and to go carefully along the path that lies ahead.

Activity: Practice using a map and compass to navigate a short trail or hike.

The goal of this activity is to familiarize yourself with using a map and compass to find your way along a short trail or hike. It will teach you the skills introduced above.

What you'll need:

- Topographic map of the area of the trail or hike
- Markers for the trail (optional)
- Things to write with (like a pencil, pen, or marker)
- For safety, a whistle
- Stopwatch or time (optional)

Instructions:

1. Start your hike at the trailhead or starting spot.
2. Use the map and guide to follow your planned route along the trail.

3. Use the compass to get bearings, measure distances, and check your position every so often.
4. If you can find them, look for trail marks or signs to help you find your way.

Want to get more detailed? Consider a waypoint challenge.

Waypoint Challenge:

1. Set up a few waypoints or signs for you to find along the trail.
2. Use your map and compass to get to each waypoint by following the coordinates or tips given.
3. At each waypoint, keep track of your progress by getting a coin or writing down a specific word.

Give Yourself a Grade

After the walk or hike is over, take a moment to think about what you learned.

Think about any problems or wins you had while using the map and compass to find your way.

Write down any questions or problems you had and, if you need to, get help or more practice.

Even though you're just practicing, it's a good idea to pack things you would normally take with you. This also helps you understand how to navigate while carrying a full backpack, which might be harder than you think. Also, the first few times, bring an adult along. That way, the two of you can figure things out together when you get stuck.

CHAPTER SEVEN: FIRST AID

Whether going on a short walk or a longer camping trip, you should always be ready for the unexpected when you're out in nature, such as taking the wrong path and getting lost. As you've learned by reading so far, you can quickly find yourself in a survival situation if you get lost in the woods. Now that you know how to build a shelter and look for food, it's time to talk about first aid skills.

Getting lost is stressful enough. Things get worse if you or the person you're with gets injured. Like with everything else, the good thing is that having basic knowledge can help you remain calm. By learning how to check for injuries, stop bleeding, and handle broken bones, you can prevent more damage and stay focused on getting rescued.

When injuries happen, it's important to quickly and correctly figure out how bad an injury is. Basic first aid skills can help with this, whether putting pressure on a wound to stop it from bleeding, making a homemade splint for a broken bone, or supporting someone in shock. These first steps can make a big difference in preventing problems from worsening and ensuring the wounded person is safe.

Pay Attention to Environmental Risks

As you've read, environmental dangers in the woods can hurt your health and safety. Having first aid skills can help you deal with heat exhaustion, hypothermia, hunger, or bites from insects or snakes. With this information, you can take steps to avoid more problems and make sure you stay healthy.

Extreme temperatures, whether hot or cold, can be dangerous. Basic first aid skills teach you to recognize and treat heat exhaustion, heatstroke, cold, and frostbite. Remember the shelter we talked about? Building one is a way to protect yourself from the weather, but there are also ways to control your body temperature that can help.

Also, the forest is home to many animals, some of which may be dangerous. Knowing how to deal with insects, spiders, snakes, and other animals that could bite or sting is very important. First-aid training teaches you how to recognize venomous species, treat bites or stings properly, and reduce the chance of more encounters.

Remain Focused

In a survival situation, the key to staying alive is to use your resources well. If you are with someone else, you also need to communicate well and realize you're a resource to each other. Just like your best friend might be good in math while you excel in English, they may remember more about certain things than you do.

First-aid skills not only help with physical needs, but they also help with emotional needs. You can improve your and your group's morale by staying calm and sure of yourself. Learning ways to deal with stress, like deep breathing movements or making a routine, can help you feel less anxious and keep a positive attitude. Remember that finding your way out of the woods is simple problem-solving; to nail the task, you must remain focused. Training in basic first aid gives you the skills to deal with a survival scenario's mental and emotional challenges. By giving yourself and others emotional support, you can boost morale, build endurance, and make it more likely that you will survive.

Beyond first aid, knowing how to make and use simple signaling tools, like homemade flags or distress signals, can help you get rescued. You might not realize that things like mirrors, flashlights, or whistles can let people know where you are and that you need help.

Now that you know the importance of learning first aid, you might wonder where to start. The best answer is to look in your community to see what first aid courses are offered. You can also find classes online with a quick search. You might even be able to find classes that are focused on first aid in the woods, depending on where you live. Talk with an adult before signing up for the classes. In the meantime, consider the following tips on how to spot infections and care for basic cuts and wounds.

TREATING BASIC CUTS

You will learn the importance of carrying a first aid kit later in this chapter. For now, let's look at the most essential steps for handling cuts. Since you won't have a fully stocked medicine cabinet, you might have to get creative to treat cuts and wounds when lost in the woods, but you can still give basic care. Here are some steps to take:

Take a moment to determine how bad the cut or wound is. You might only need a little care if it's just a tiny cut or scrape. But if the cut is deeper or bleeding, you'll need to go to the next step.

If the wound is bleeding heavily, try to put direct pressure on it with any clean cloth or clothes you have with you. Press down hard and steady for a few minutes or until the blood slows or stops. Putting the cut above your heart level can also help stop the bleeding.

If you have clean water, rinse the wound with it. Let the water run over the wound to clean it and get rid of any dirt, debris, or germs. **If you don't have much water**, try to gently wipe away dust and dirt with a clean cloth or towel.

Cover the cut with a clean cloth, a bandage, or anything else that is clean and sterile. If you don't have one, try to make one out of any clean fabric or clothes you have. Make sure the bandage is big enough to cover the whole cut, and use tape, string, or a tight knot to keep it in place.

Keep the injured area elevated to reduce swelling and help the body heal if you can. The less you move the injured part, the better. This helps avoid further damage and lets the wound heal without being bothered. Depending on where the injury is, this may be difficult, but being mindful of your actions is a good idea.

Remember that these steps are meant to give basic first aid in an emergency. Always bring a first-aid kit, even if you only plan on spending a short time in the woods. You never know when you or someone else might need care.

WATCH FOR SIGNS OF INFECTION

In a survival situation, even minor cuts can quickly become dangerous infections. When you know first aid, you can take care of cuts correctly. When cleaned and bandaged well, they are less likely to get infected and will heal faster. Speaking of that, sometimes it's hard to tell if a cut or wound is infected, but there are a few things you can look for.

Increased pain: If the pain around the cut worsens over time instead of better, this could be a sign of an infection.

Redness and swelling: The wound might be infected if the area around the cut gets red and swollen.

Pay attention to how it feels: If the skin around the cut feels hot to the touch and warmer than the rest of your skin, it could be a sign of an infection.

Pus or slimy stuff: This sounds gross — and it kind of is — but it's still an important tip. If you see yellow or green liquid coming out of the cut, it could point to an infection.

Does the cut smell? Again — gross — but if the cut smells bad, there is most likely an infection.

Slow healing: There may be an infection if the cut isn't getting better or healing as it should.

Feeling sick: If you or the person with the cut gets a fever, chills, or just feels sick in addition to the wound, this could be a sign that the infection has spread.

If you notice any of these signs, try not to panic. Panicking makes it hard to focus, and in these situations, focus is critical. Now that you know the bare minimum, let's look at some more specific situations.

TREATING COMMON INJURIES IN THE WILDERNESS

The best-case scenario is that you never get lost hiking in the woods. The next best case is that you don't get injured if lost. In the event both things happen, knowing how to identify and treat the most common issues will help you stay calm and focused. We've already talked about cuts and wounds, so let's look at other things that might happen.

Sprains

A sprain occurs when you injure a ligament, a type of tissue that holds bones together at a joint. Most of the time, a sprain happens when a joint is pushed into an odd position, and the ligament is stretched or torn. There are a few things that can cause sprains when you go hiking in the woods:

Uneven ground: The trails in the woods can sometimes be rocky. If you step on something unstable, you could twist your ankle or knee.

Falling or tripping: Tree branches or hidden holes can make you trip or fall in the woods. You can sprain a joint if you hit it or twist it while falling.

Exhaustion: Hiking is a workout. If you push yourself too hard, you might get tired. Keeping your balance can be tricky when that happens, and you might be more likely to trip and fall, leading to a possible sprain.

Carrying your backpack: If you're hiking and have a heavy pack or other gear, it can throw you off balance. Your joints are more likely to get sprained because the extra weight puts more pressure on them. It might sound silly, but practicing walking around your house or yard with a full pack before you head into the woods can help you get used to the weight.

To avoid injuries while hiking, you should:

Wear good shoes. Sturdy hiking boots with good grip that support your feet are best. With the right shoes, your feet will be more stable and less likely to twist.

Use walking sticks. Walking sticks can help you keep your balance and support you while hiking. They also take some of the weight off your joints, which can help prevent injury.

Be careful and pay attention. Look for rocks, tree roots, and uneven ground on the path. Take your time and watch where you're putting your feet.

Warm up and stretch. Before hiking, do some light movements and stretches to get your muscles ready. This makes you more flexible and makes it less likely that you'll pull something.

Don't push yourself too hard. Take breaks and rest. During your hike, stop often to rest and let your muscles heal.

If you get a sprain while hiking or camping, it can be painful, swell up, and make moving hard. Try to rest the hurt area and keep it elevated as much as possible. If you packed an ice pack in your first aid kit, you might also need to use it.

Bug bites and stings: All sorts of bugs can bite and sting in nature. This can make you itch, swell, hurt, or even have an allergic reaction. If you get bitten or stung, try to remove the stinger or insect if it's still there. Clean the area as well as possible and put an ice pack on it to reduce swelling. If you have anti-itch ointment in your backpack, you can also use that on the area.

Heat exhaustion or heat stroke: When spending time outdoors, it's essential to be aware of heat-related illnesses like heat exhaustion and heat stroke. Heat exhaustion and heat stroke can happen if you're in hot weather for too long and don't drink enough water. This can cause you to sweat and feel weak, dizzy, and sick. If you can, move somewhere cooler, find water, and rest. Heatstroke can quickly become a medical emergency with signs like a high body temperature, confusion, seizures, and fainting. If you notice yourself feeling weak or dizzy, stop what you're doing and rest.

Dehydration: You might not realize it, but dehydration can happen whether it's hot outside or not. When your body doesn't have enough water, you get dehydrated. Dehydration can make you feel thirsty, have a dry mouth, be tired or dizzy, or go to the bathroom less. If you feel any of these, rest in the shade and slowly drink water.

Hypothermia: You can get hypothermia if you're in cold weather for too long, especially if you get wet. When you have hypothermia, it means your body is losing heat more quickly than it can make it. Some signs are shaking, feeling confused, tired, and having trouble moving. If you notice these signs, wrap yourself warmly and remove your wet clothes.

Being prepared for anything is key to hiking in the woods. Part of that preparation is having a first aid kit in your backpack. But where do you start? What are the most important things to pack that won't make your backpack heavier than it already is? Keep reading to find out.

IMPORTANCE OF CARRYING A FIRST AID KIT

You've probably realized by now that having a first aid kit when hiking in the woods is essential. A good first aid kit can help treat minor injuries and even save your life in an emergency. Nature can be hard to predict, and falls, or injuries can happen even on the calmest, best-planned hiking trips. With a well-stocked first aid kit, you can help yourself or others until professional help arrives. Consider the following reasons why it's crucial to carry a first-aid kit when hiking.

Hiking paths can be dangerous because of uneven ground, slippery surfaces, and wildlife. Injuries like cuts, scrapes, sprains, or bruises can quickly happen, no matter how cautious you are. With a first aid kit, you can take care of these issues right away, reducing the chance of infection and other problems.

If you have a deep cut or are bleeding a lot, a first aid kit can help you stop the bleeding until you get additional medical help. Wounds can be cleaned and dressed with bandages, gauze pads, adhesive tape, and antiseptic solutions. These treatments can keep wounds from getting infected and help them heal.

You might also encounter insects, poisonous plants, or other things that can cause allergic responses when hiking in the woods. Antihistamines, creams for bug bites or stings, and medicines for allergies or anaphylaxis in your first aid kit can help you deal with these situations. If you know you're allergic to certain things, you will need to be extra careful while hiking.

Additionally, hiking can be strenuous on your body, and even minor injuries or strains can wear you out. Pain relievers like ibuprofen or acetaminophen can remove pain and decrease swelling, so you can keep going or return home safely. Hikers with health problems like asthma, diabetes, or heart problems should bring the medicines they need in their first aid kit. In case of an emergency, these medicines should be easy to get.

When hiking, accidents like twisted ankles or broken bones can happen. A first aid kit should have splints, triangular bandages, and elastic wraps to keep hurt limbs from moving and stabilize them. This keeps the injury from getting worse and makes it less painful.

The exact items in a first-aid kit will depend on the hiker's needs and the length of the trip, but here are some essentials to include:

- Bandages in different sizes
- Clean cotton pads
- Medical tape
- Antiseptic solutions or wipes
- Tweezers
- Scissors and safety pins
- Disposable gloves
- CPR mask or face shield

- Painkillers like ibuprofen or acetaminophen
- Antihistamines and creams
- Stretchy wraps to immobilize and support injuries
- Specific medication for your needs
- A basic first aid guidebook

Remember that the first aid kit is only helpful if you know how to use the items in it. As mentioned earlier, taking a class in person or online can help you feel better prepared. You can also practice the first-aid skills you learn before hiking to increase your confidence.

Activity: Practice basic first aid skills, such as treating cuts and scrapes.

Once you've taken a basic first aid course, enlist your friends and family to help you practice.

What You'll Need:

- First-aid bag (with bandages, antiseptic wipes, tape, and sterile dressings)
- Different kinds of fake wounds, like cut-out paper forms or bandages
- Water and soap to wash your hands
- Disposable gloves
- A clock or timer
- A first aid guide

Instructions:

1. Set up a place that will be the "First Aid Station." Put everything in a neat pile and ensure it's easy to get to.

2. Gather everyone and briefly explain why you need to practice and how they can help. Making it a game will be more enjoyable for everyone. Ask an adult to help you set this up.
3. Explain that the goal of the game is to practice using the first aid kit to treat cuts and scrapes.
4. Remember to start by washing your hands or using hand sanitizer.
5. Explain what each part of the first aid kit is for and how it works. Talk briefly about how important it is to check the wound, clean it properly, and put on the proper covering. Talking about these things will help you retain what you've learned.
6. Bring out the fake wounds or bandages and place them randomly on different parts of each participant's body, like their arm, leg, or hand.
7. Have your friends and family pair up.
8. Set a five-minute timer and tell everyone to take turns being the "first aider" and the "patient." The first aider should look at the cut, clean it with antiseptic wipes, put on the proper bandages, and, if necessary, tape them down.
9. After the set amount of time, get everyone together for a review session. Talk about common problems, good solutions, and anything else important they learned during the task.

This might seem silly, but it's good information for everyone to have, whether they plan to go hiking with you or not. Plus, they might use a technique that you've not seen but would help you handle the situation better.

CHAPTER EIGHT: COMMUNICATION

Being lost in the woods can be a scary thing to go through. But it's important to stay calm and know you can get help. You can significantly improve your chances of being found if you keep your mind clear and use basic survival skills. Follow the steps below to stay safe and find help quickly.

Stop and Assess Your Situation

When you realize you're lost, the first thing you should do is stop walking. Take a moment to calm down and catch your breath. Look around for known signs or landmarks that could help you find your way back. If you have a compass or a map, you can use them to find your way. Remember that getting scared and walking around aimlessly can make it harder for rescuers to find you.

Stay Visible

If you're lost, it's usually best to stay in one place, especially if you're not sure where you are. When you move around, finding you can be more challenging for search teams. Find a safe place away from dangers like high cliffs or bodies of water to make it easier for people to find you. You can do this by making a warning fire, using a whistle, or tying brightly colored clothes to a tree. Continue reading to learn more about visual and audible clues that can help people find you.

Using Visual Clues

When you're lost in the woods, it is necessary to make a distress signal to increase the likelihood of being located. To start, you can use brightly colored clothes or materials like plastic bags or tarps to make a visible marker on the ground or fasten them to a tree.

You might also use the smoke from a fire, which can be observed from a considerable distance. When using this method, monitor the fire and only put it in a safe area. In addition, making an SOS sign or an arrow out of rocks or logs can help people find you if they're using a drone or helicopter. You'll need to put this signal in an open area so it can be found easily.

Mirrors are also efficient for reflecting sunshine toward people who can help. To use a mirror, hold it horizontally in one hand and direct the reflection toward the object you want to see. This can be done by tilting the mirror to face the sun and adjusting the reflection to land in the appropriate position. When lost in the woods, having a mirror in your backpack is helpful because they are small, lightweight, and easy to carry and use.

You can also use a flashlight and Morse code to send for help. This is a simple and effective way to talk when you can't or are trying to help someone find you. Morse code is a system of dots and dashes that can be sent as light messages by turning on and off a flashlight in a certain way. To use Morse code with a flashlight, you need to know the Morse code alphabet, which comprises short and long signs. The dot shows a short signal or a quick flash, while the dash shows a longer signal or a flash that lasts longer. Each letter and number have its own pattern.

Here are some examples of Morse code and the flashlight signs that go with them:

- The letter "S" is shown by three short signs (dot-dot-dot);
- The letter "O" is shown by three longer signals: a dash, a dash, and another dash;

- Repeat the "S" signal again, and you know the universal "SOS" request for help.

Send your message one letter at a time, with a short break between each one. Leave more time between words to tell them apart. A space in Morse code is shown by a pause the same length as three dots.

Using Morse code with a flashlight can be an excellent way to communicate, especially in emergencies. Remember to practice beforehand and learn the basic alphabet and popular phrases.

Using Audible Clues

The most obvious way to get help is to use your voice by shouting or yelling regularly. However, this can hurt your voice after a while, so be mindful of when and where you use this method. You could also use a whistle, which might be louder than your voice and save your throat from discomfort.

To use a whistle, find a location with a high probability of reaching a person who can help, such as an open clearing. The international signal for distress consists of three quick blows on a whistle, repeated at regular intervals. Repeating this process for extended lengths of time while pausing periodically to pay attention to potential responses is recommended. Whistles are helpful tools because of their ability to transmit sound across long distances, even in situations with a dense forest.

You could also use a stick or rock to hit a tree trunk to make loud noises that might draw attention. Remember to take breaks between signs to listen for answers or sounds from search teams.

Using Location Devices

In addition to using the above signals, you might also consider buying a Personal Locator Beacon (PLB) or an Emergency Position-Indicating Radio Beacon (EPIRB). These tools are made to send out signs and help rescuers find you quickly. They are typically expensive and not something you could buy on your own, but you might talk with an adult to see how you could earn the money, especially if you plan to spend a lot of time hiking. If you're able to purchase one, follow the tips below to help you use it.

Stay cool and look at the situation. Panicking can make it hard to make good decisions and think clearly. Take a moment to gather your thoughts and look around you. Look for signs or locations that can help you figure out where you are.

Put your alerting device to work: PLBs and EPIRBs usually have a button or switch that can be used to send out an emergency signal. When you're ready to send the danger signal, press or toggle the distress button.

Place the device correctly: Make sure that the antenna of the device is not blocked by things like thick vegetation or trees that could interfere with the signal. For the best signal range, you should hold the device or put it on higher ground.

Wait for the signal to be sent: Once the signaling device is turned on, it will start sending a distress signal via satellite or radio, based on the device. This signal includes your unique identification code and location information.

Stay in an open area: If you can, move to a space or an open area while you wait for help. This makes it more likely that search and rescue teams will hear your signal. Avoid dense tree growth or deep valleys that might impede signal transmission.

Save your battery power: Use the device as little as possible to keep it working until help comes. Turn it off when you're not sending signals, but don't forget to turn it on every so often to see if the search and rescue teams have sent you any texts or news.

Follow the steps for your device: Each signaling device may have its own features or extra functions. Read the instructions ahead of time to understand how to use it, fix problems, or maintain the device.

Signal continuity: If you can, keep it with you even after you turn it on. Rescuers could use tools that help them figure out where the signal is coming from. If you move away from the device, it might be harder for them to find you.

Respond to attempts to talk to you: Once search and rescue teams get your distress signal, they may try to talk to you. Be ready to answer their calls, texts, or any other way they might try to get in touch with you. Tell them everything they need to know about your state, your injuries, and any changes.

Remember that signaling devices are useful tools, but they should not be used instead of proper planning and skills for living in the woods. It's important to tell other people about your hiking plans, bring tools to help you find your way, and learn some basic outdoor safety skills. When you go out into the woods, stay safe and come prepared.

Staying positive and keeping your spirits up while waiting for help is crucial. Remind yourself that help is coming and that you've taken the proper steps to make it more likely that you'll be found. Take breaks often to rest and keep your energy up. If you have food, divide it into small amounts and eat often to maintain your energy. Use your resources wisely to make sure you have enough until help comes. Do things that help you stay upbeat and on track, like singing or meditating.

If you get lost in the woods, you need to stay calm and follow your plan. You can increase your chances of being found if you stop and take stock of the situation. Remember to tell someone ahead of time where to look for you if you don't come back on time from hiking or camping. Being ready and knowing how to survive can make a big difference in safely getting you back to your friends and family.

Activity: Practice making distress signals and assessing how easy they are to see or hear.

Practicing distress signs if you get lost in the woods is vital. Plus, practicing will help you feel more confident if you ever need the signals in real life. When practicing, have a friend or an adult with you to tell you what you could improve and ensure they get the signal.

Learn and practice common signals: As mentioned above, three short whistle blows will alert people that you are in need. Additionally, three fires, smoke columns, or three reflective signals from a mirror or flashlight will also do the trick. These signs are easy for most people to understand and can help get help in an emergency.

Practice with all the tools: Make sure you have the right tools for signaling when you practice. Learning how to use each one will increase your comfort and your knowledge.

Choose an open area: Find a place that is safe and open, away from things that could be dangerous, like hills, steep slopes, or lots of plants. This will let you practice without danger and ensure your signs can be seen or heard.

Prepare for visual signals: If you want to practice visual signals, go somewhere open where you can see well. You can use an open space, the top of a hill, or the edge of a lake or river. Make sure your chosen signaling tools are easy to get to.

Practice sending audible signals: If you want to practice sending audible signals, pick a place where the sound will travel well. Stand in an open area and make three short sounds or whistle blows with a short pause between each one. You can use a whistle or something else that makes a loud noise.

Practice making visual signals: Use the tools you picked to make the distress signal. For example, if you have a mirror, you could catch the sun and reflect it toward a goal or an area where you want to draw attention. Repeat the signal three times, pausing for a short time between each signal.

Observe your surroundings: After you've signaled, take a moment to look around. Listen and look for any signs of movement or response. In an actual situation, it's essential to stay alert and ready to help if anyone comes along.

Repeat and improve: Practice often to get comfortable and skilled. Try out different methods and tools for signals to see which ones work best for you. Think about things like the weather, the terrain, and the tools you have.

Remember that you should only use distress signs when your safety or the safety of others is in danger. It is essential to know the rules and regulations about distress signals in your area and any unique signals that may be used there.

CHAPTER NINE: WEATHER AWARENESS

Importance of Being Aware

Imagine you're lost in the woods, with tall trees and strange paths around you. The sun is going down, and you don't know how to return home. In this dangerous situation, it can be imperative for you to know what the weather is doing. Being aware of the weather can help you make smart choices, stay safe, and increase your chances of being found or finding your way back. Remember, you might not have a cellular signal, so simply hitting the weather app on your phone won't give you the necessary information. Consider the following before heading to the trails.

TEMPERATURE AND CLOTHING

The weather affects the temperature, and if you don't know how the temperature changes, it can be tough to take the steps you need to take to succeed in survival situations. The weather can change quickly in the woods, especially when the seasons change. If you're lost and don't know where you are, knowing whether it is likely to get colder or warmer can help you prepare by deciding how to dress. Dressing correctly can keep you from getting cold, which happens when your body loses heat faster than it can make it, heat exhaustion, or other illnesses caused by the weather.

What you wear depends on where you live, the season, and even the time of day, but there are some typical guidelines for what you should and shouldn't wear.

Comfortable clothing. Wear loose, comfortable clothing that will allow you to move and climb about freely. The exception to this might be if you choose to wear leggings, but if you do that, make sure they are made of durable fabric that can withstand getting caught on things like branches with thorns. The nice thing about leggings is they are one of the most lightweight things you can wear – and yes, anyone can wear them. They are also made of breathable fabric, which is critical when doing anything physical.

Avoid 100% cotton garments. Although cotton might seem like a good choice since it's typically considered comfortable, it will soak up excess sweat or rain and takes a long time to dry. Think about the last time you went to an amusement park and rode the log ride. Were you wearing cotton, like denim? How long did it take to dry? Now think about the additional weight added when you're wet, and you'll understand why your cotton clothes should be left at home.

Wear layers. Layer your clothing so you can add or subtract things depending on how warm or cool you get. This way, you should be covered for typical temperature swings.

Proper footwear. Don't confuse tennis shoes with hiking boots, and don't assume one can double for the other. When choosing hiking boots, you need to try on a few, check out reviews, and go with the ones that feel good, not necessarily the ones that match your favorite hiking attire. In addition, wear them before your trek in the woods to get used to them. Breaking out new footwear on the day of the hike isn't a good idea.

Wear white or lighter colors. This is especially smart in the warmer months, as lighter colors reflect heat better. You should also consider your surroundings and have something with high visibility either on you or in your backpack to make you more visible if you get lost or injured, as people will be looking for you.

DIFFERENT WEATHER

Rain, snow, and shelter: When you're lost, bad weather like rain or snow can make things harder. Heavy rain can make it hard to get around in dense woods, and snow can make it harder for rescuers to find you if your tracks are covered. It's important to pay attention to weather reports because they can help you plan and find or make a place to stay out of the weather. Having a good place to stay dry and warm can help you stay safe until help comes.

Lightning and storms: Thunderstorms can be dangerous, and if you're out in the open during a lightning storm, you could get hit by lightning. If you look for signs of storms, like dark clouds, or thunder in the distance, you can take cover in a low-lying area away from tall trees or open fields. Lightning can travel through the ground, so staying away from open places is essential when it's storming.

Wind and navigation: Wind can help you figure out how to get back home or find a place where you can get help. If you pay attention to the wind blowing, you can figure out where it is coming from and use that to help you find your way. Also, the wind can affect how fast a fire spreads, so it's important to be careful when lighting a fire or sending a signal.

Visibility and signaling: Fog, heavy rain, or snowfall can make it hard to see, making it harder for rescuers to find you and for you to find your way. If you know the weather, you can decide when it's best to stay put and wait for help and when it might be better to try to find your way out of the woods. In an emergency, using brightly colored clothes, whistles, or other warning tools can work better when people can see them.

When you're lost in the woods, it's vital that you know what the weather is like. It helps you make good choices, stay safe and make it more likely that you will be found or find your way back home. Now that you know why it's important to be aware, let's look at how you can be a mini meteorologist and predict weather changes.

PREDICTING WEATHER CHANGES

You've checked the weather for days before the hike and are prepared thanks to the tips above, but what happens when the weather changes? Can you predict that? When going into the woods, it's essential to be ready and know how the weather changes to keep yourself safe. Even though it's impossible to know exactly how the weather will change, you can use many ways and tools to stay aware and make smart choices.

Not to sound like a broken record, but checking the forecast before you leave should always be the first step. Use a local weather forecast from a reliable source, such as a meteorological service or a reputable weather app. Listen to any tips or alerts that are sent out for your area. But keep in mind that weather predictions aren't always correct, especially in remote areas, so it's essential to be on the lookout.

Once you head into the woods, take the time to glance up and watch the clouds and sky around you. Changes in cloud shapes, colors, and how they move can tell us a lot about how the weather will be. For instance, dark, tall clouds often mean a storm is coming, while high, wispy clouds may mean the weather will be nice. Learn to spot the different kinds of clouds and the weather patterns that go with them to improve your understanding.

You should also pay attention to where and how fast the wind blows. A quick change in the wind's direction or a significant increase in speed could mean a storm is coming. Remember that the local landscape can change how the wind blows, so pay attention to your surroundings. If you're in a valley where the wind can't typically be felt, check out the trees above to see how the wind affects them.

One of the best tools to have with you is a barometer. A barometer records the pressure in the air, which can tell you a lot about upcoming changes in the weather. When the pressure drops, it usually means that a low-pressure system and possibly bad weather are coming. On the other hand, rising pressure is often a sign of good weather. You can buy a small or handheld barometer that you can take into the woods with you at most outdoor stores. Before heading out, take the time to understand how to use the barometer. While some might be different, the typical steps are listed below.

1. Get familiar with the barometer by learning its features, controls, and display. This is done by reading the user manual or directions that came with it.

2. If necessary, calibrate the barometer by following the directions in the manual. The reference level may need to be changed, or a baseline pressure may need to be set.

3. Practice using it by choosing a place that is typical of the area or region where you want to measure the pressure of the air. Stay away from places with strong drafts or those that are right next to heat sources.

4. Make sure you have a firm grip on the handheld barometer. Keep the device away from your face to keep the numbers from being affected by your breath or the humidity.

5. To determine how much pressure is in the air, look at the barometer's display or gauge. The device may show the pressure in different units, such as inches of mercury (inHg) or millibars (bar). Make sure you know what kind of unit is being used.

6. Write down the current air pressure and keep track of the value so you can look at it or use it in the future. Compare it to what the pressure is like when the weather changes.

Watch how animals act. Animals are often more sensitive to weather changes than people are. Pay attention to how birds, insects, and other animals in the woods act. If they quickly get quiet, hide, or do something strange, it could mean that the weather is about to change. Even though this method isn't perfect, it can give you more information to help you figure out what the weather will be like.

Educate yourself. Learn about the weather trends in the area you're visiting. Some places tend to get certain kinds of weather, like quick thunderstorms, localized microbursts, or sudden temperature changes. If you know the area's climate, you'll be better able to predict and prepare for bad weather.

Be prepared. Especially in wooded places, the weather can change quickly. Be prepared with rain gear and a possible change of clothes. It's better to be too ready than to be caught off guard by sudden changes in the weather.

Remember that figuring out how the weather will change is an ongoing process, and it's vital to keep evaluating the situations around you. Use a combination of these methods to improve your chances of predicting weather changes while you're in the woods. If you can pay attention to your surroundings, you can get out of the woods before the weather turns.

STAYING DRY

To stay dry and warm in the woods, it's important to be ready for different kinds of weather. Pay attention to the following tips to help you out.

Rainy Weather

When it's raining, the most important thing is to stay dry. Start by putting on the right clothes, like a jacket and pants, that are waterproof. These will help keep you dry and keep the rain away.

Also, choose base layers of materials that wick away moisture, like synthetic fabrics or wool. These materials pull sweat away from your body. Bring a waterproof cover for your backpack or dry bags to keep your things safe and dry.

Depending on your situation, taking cover might be a good idea until the rain passes. Look for natural cover, like big trees or rocky outcroppings, to keep you safe. You can also use a tarp or a rainfly to make a makeshift cover if you need to. Ensure it's at an angle so water can run off when it rains. Putting extra socks and shoes in a waterproof bag is another good idea. Also, dry shoes can make a big difference in how warm and cozy your feet stay.

Cold Weather

When it's cold outside, it's important to stay warm and insulate your body. By wearing layers, you can keep warm air close to your body. Start with a moisture-wicking base layer, add a warm middle layer like a fleece or a down jacket, and finish with a waterproof and windproof top layer. Remember to wear a hat, gloves, and warm socks to protect your head, hands, and feet.

Start a fire and gather dry wood to keep warm if you can. The heat from the fire will help fight off the cold. Don't forget to bring a protective case with a lighter or matches.

Regardless of the weather, staying hydrated and eating well is essential. Keep your energy up by drinking lots of water and eating high-energy snacks like granola bars or trail mix. Using these tips, you'll be better prepared to stay dry and warm in the woods, making your time outside more pleasant and comfortable. Always put safety first and be aware of what's happening around you.

Activity: Monitor weather conditions for a week and create a chart to track changes in temperature, precipitation, and wind speed. If you've purchased a barometer, get used to it by using the steps above and the instructions in the manual. Test yourself by comparing your notes to what the weather forecast says. It's also a good idea to pay close attention to the area you plan to go hiking in if it isn't the same area where you live.

CHAPTER TEN:
MENTAL
TOUGHNESS

Techniques for Mental Toughness in Survival Situations

If you get lost in the woods, you need to stay calm and in control. Take deep breaths to slow your heart rate and clear your mind. Also, don't be too hard on yourself. Yes, you've read the book and practiced, but that doesn't mean you won't panic just a bit if you do get lost. Give yourself a moment to validate your feelings, then focus on what you need to do next.

When lost, remember everything you've learned and work to get yourself to safety. Lastly, trust yourself. Using these methods, you can build the mental toughness you need to handle whatever situation arises.

STAYING POSITIVE AND MOTIVATED

It's one thing to tell yourself to stay positive and another thing to do it, especially in a scary situation like being lost in the woods. The following tips are great for life in general, whether or not you're stuck in the woods.

Stay calm. The first step is to stop being scared and anxious. Take some deep breaths and try to calm down. If you're scared, you won't be able to make good decisions or think clearly.

Check out your surroundings. Look around you and think about the things you can use. Look for water, a place to stay, and food. If you know what's going on, you can plan, which naturally helps you calm down.

Set small goals that you can reach. Break your situation down into small jobs that you can do. This could mean finding a place to get water, making a place to stay, or getting firewood. By reaching these smaller goals, you'll feel like you're progressing and staying motivated.

Focus on the here and now. Focus on the things you need to do. Keep your mind on your immediate wants and work step by step to meet them.

Stay optimistic by talking to yourself. How you think is significant in how positive and motivated you can be. Positive self-talk can help you feel better. Remind yourself that you can do things and can find solutions. Believe in yourself and tell yourself you can handle your problems.

Problem-solve. Instead of thinking about your problems, put your energy into finding answers. Use the things you have in a creative and helpful way. Taking part in activities that help you solve problems will keep your mind busy and help you keep in a good mood.

Make sure you take care of your body: Your mental and emotional state has a lot to do with how your body feels. Keep drinking water, eat whatever food you find, and try to rest. Taking care of your physical needs will help you stay strong and determined.

Connect with nature. That may seem like the last thing you want to do since you're lost in nature, but taking deep breaths to center yourself is crucial. So yes, look around and breathe deeply.

Find purpose and meaning. Even in a survival situation, it can be important to keep going if you can find purpose and meaning. Think about your goals, dreams, and what's important to you. Keep in touch with your goals and let them lead you forward.

Remember that in a survival scenario, your chances of getting through are much better if you stay positive and motivated. To overcome problems and find your way back to safety, you need to be able to adapt, be strong, and be determined.

Activity: Practice mindfulness techniques, such as deep breathing or meditation, to stay calm and focused in stressful situations. You can find information about mindfulness and guided meditations through apps and videos you find online. One quick technique you can use to calm yourself is detailed below.

Deep breathing is an effective way to help you feel calm and relaxed. Here are some easy steps to help you learn to breathe deeply and stay calm:

1. Find a quiet, comfortable place where you won't be disturbed.
2. Sit or lie down in a way that lets your body fully relax.
3. Close your eyes to tune out outside noises and focus on yourself.
4. Take a few regular breaths in through your nose and a slow, soft breath out through your mouth.
5. Pay attention to how your breath feels as it enters and leaves your body.
6. Once you've done this a few times, lengthen your breath. Take a slow, controlled breath through your nose. Your stomach should rise as your lungs fill with air. Try to count slowly for 4–6 seconds.
7. Let your breath out slowly and evenly through your mouth for 4-6 seconds. Gently pulling in your stomach will help you completely empty your lungs.
8. Continue the cycle of deep breathing by taking deep breaths in and slowly letting them out. Keep the beat steady and easy.

9. As you continue to take deep breaths, let go of any thoughts or fears that are getting in the way. Keep your mind on the present and only think about your breath.
10. Practice for 5–10 minutes. As you get used to it, you can slowly add more time to your practice sessions.

To get the most out of this practice, try to make deep breathing a part of your daily routine. You can do it in the morning to get your day off on a calm note, or you can use it to deal with stress when things are hard. Deep breathing is a skill that gets better the more you do it. Doing this exercise regularly can help you feel calmer and more relaxed in your daily life.

CHAPTER ELEVEN: EMERGENCY SITUATIONS

We've talked a lot about getting lost in the woods and what to do, but did you know these same techniques can be applied to other emergencies? That's right. You can apply much of what you've learned to help your friends and family when things like natural disasters or other emergencies happen. Think about everything you've learned and consider the following tips.

Stay calm: As you've learned, staying calm and collected is the most important thing. Thinking clearly and making good choices can be tricky when you're scared. Try to stay calm and take a deep breath.

Stay informed: Use reliable sources, such as local authorities, news stations, or weather apps, to discover what's happening with the emergency. This helps you learn what kind of disaster you are facing and what steps you should take.

Have an emergency kit: Remember the emergency kit you put together for exploring the woods? This is almost the same thing. Put together an emergency kit with water, non-perishable food, a flashlight, batteries, a first aid kit, extra clothes, a phone charger, and any necessary medicines. Put the kit somewhere that is easy to get to.

Follow directions: Listen carefully to what the local government, emergency services, or community leaders say. Follow the advice to leave, stay put, or do whatever else is given to make sure your safety.

Stay in touch: When these things happen, you might not be able to get to your family right away. Let them know where you are and that you're okay if possible. Limit your phone use, especially if the emergency causes the power to go out. Use text messages or social media to talk when you can because they are often more effective in emergencies.

Stay away from dangers: Watch out for things like downed power lines, damaged buildings, and flooded places that could be dangerous.

Help other people: If it is safe to do so, help those in need, especially children, older people, and people with disabilities. Help as much as possible, but don't put yourself in danger.

Stay together: If you are with your family or friends during an emergency, stay together and create a plan in case you get split. Keep an eye out for each other and make sure everyone is safe.

The effects of an emergency or natural disaster may last for a while. Be ready for things like power outages, running out of supplies, or changes to your regular routine. Stay calm, and don't give up. Reach out for help if you feel stressed or worried after the emergency. Talking to a trusted adult, a friend, or other support to help you process your feelings about what happened. Always keep in mind that your safety and the safety of others is the most essential thing in an emergency. By staying calm, informed, and ready, you can react well to a natural disaster and help lessen its effects.

HAVING AN
EMERGENCY PLAN

Having a plan for a disaster is very important because it keeps people safe when bad things happen out of the blue. Additionally, having a plan ready can make a big difference. It helps you know what to do quickly and effectively, which can save lives.

Remember when we talked about remaining calm? Having a plan helps you with this. Focusing on staying calm and problem-solving is much easier when you don't have to start from square one. In the event of a natural disaster or other emergency, follow the plan, and remember to breathe to help calm yourself.

A disaster plan is also important because it helps everyone work together. During an emergency, sharing knowledge, asking for help, and working as a team is essential. Usually, an emergency plan has important phone numbers and places to meet so everyone knows who to call and where to go. Good communication keeps your friends and family from doing the same things twice, makes sure you use your resources wisely and helps everyone react better. For instance, maybe your grandparent lives in the same town. In an emergency, your parents will want to ensure their safety. Your job in that situation might be to take care of a sibling or help gather what you need for your emergency kit, if it isn't already made, while they contact your grandparent.

In addition, remember the activities you've completed in this book. They were to help you prepare in case you got lost. Your family can prepare for an emergency by doing some things. Practice helps you learn what to do and can find ways to make things better. Your family will gain the skills, information, and confidence they need to handle emergencies when they practice. Practicing also helps you figure out where everyone's skills lie. Your younger siblings might not be able to do what you can, but they can collect blankets or some other activity suited for their age and developmental level. It's also important to understand that different situations need different responses, and a good plan considers things like disabilities, medical conditions, and more. A good plan ensures everyone is cared for and included when a disaster strikes.

In short, it's vital to have an emergency plan because it keeps the ones closest to you safe, helps everyone work together, makes everyone prepared, and considers their needs. By putting time and effort into creating and practicing a plan, you and your family will be better prepared.

STAYING SAFE AND FINDING HELP

While your family should have a plan for emergencies, there are a few key things for you to know and plan for, depending on where you are and the emergency. Just like planning for survival in the wilderness, you might pack certain things depending on the weather and who you're with. Pay attention to the strategies below to help you stay safe and get help in a disaster. Following them can make a big difference in the outcome.

Also, depending on who you're with, you might be better prepared for emergency situations thanks to the practice you've already completed. This is good to know if you're with friends or your younger siblings. There may be times when staying calm is even more important if you find yourself in charge. We've talked about this a lot, but it really is one of the most important things. It's normal to feel all sorts of things, from fear to stress, in an emergency, but finding your center of calm must be the first focus. Remember your breathing techniques and center yourself. This allows you to assess the situation and start problem-solving. Pro tip? The more you practice deep breathing, the easier it will be to find your calm.

Know where the emergency exits are. Whether you're at school, in a mall, or anywhere else, you should know where the emergency exits are. Note the closest exits and other ways out in case one is closed. If you know how to get out, you can do it quickly and easily.

Get help. If you have a major emergency, call emergency services right away. In the United States, this means calling 911. You should also have a list of important phone numbers, like those of your parents, guardian, or other trusted adults who can help you, on your phone or memorized. In an emergency, it's important to let other people know where you are and if there are any possible risks. If you're stuck or hurt, try calling for help or texting to let people know what's happening. You can also use social media or apps to contact people you know in an emergency.

Follow the safety rules. There are different ways to handle different kinds of situations. "Stop, drop, and roll" if your clothes catch fire in a fire, and crawl low under the smoke to get out. "Drop, cover, and hold on" during a quake by getting under a strong piece of furniture. Understanding safety rules and following them can save lives.

Find a safe place to stay and stay together. If you are caught in bad weather or a dangerous situation, find a safe place to stay right away. Move to a safe place away from windows, and if you can, hide in a strong building or one of the marked safe areas. Stay with your teachers, friends, or family to make sure that everyone is safe.

Trust your feelings. In an emergency, your instincts can be very useful tools. If you get the feeling that something is wrong or dangerous, go with your gut and move accordingly. Also, if you see someone who needs help and it is safe to do so, you should help them or tell the right people.

Always keep in mind that accidents can happen at any time, so you need to be ready and know what to do. Practice these techniques and talk about them with your family, friends, and teachers to make sure that everyone is well-informed and ready to handle unexpected scenarios. The most important thing should always be your safety and well-being.

Activity: Create an emergency plan for your family and practice executing it. A general plan for emergencies includes a lot of the things we've already talked about, plus a few others. When creating the plan, get the whole family involved. They may have ideas that you've not thought about.

Plan for communication: Set up an effective way for family members to talk to each other. This could mean picking a place to meet, choosing a primary and secondary point of contact outside of the local area, and coming up with other ways to talk, like text messages or social media.

Contacts for emergencies: Make a list of people you can call in an emergency, such as local officials, hospitals, the police, the fire department, and your utility company. Make sure that everyone in the family has a copy of this list.

Consider evacuation: Plan your evacuation and decide on a safe place for your family to go in case you need to leave your home. It's important to have a few different ideas in case one is blocked or unsafe. Think about each family member and plan accordingly. You might have family members living with you who are older or have a younger sibling who will need help.

Setting up plans for staying at home during an emergency: There might be times when you can't leave the home and need to shelter in place. For this situation, pre-planning is key. It's good to have a space in eh home where you've stored things such as food, drink, medicine, and batteries. This can include any emergency kit that you've already prepared as well.

Plan for your pets: If you have pets, make sure they have food, drink, medicine, leashes, and ID tags in case of an emergency. Find shelters or hotels that allow pets in case you need to leave your home.

Practice: Run through your plan with your family often. Do fire drills, evacuation drills, and any other preparation to make sure everyone knows what to do in an emergency.

Make sure to review and update your emergency plan on a regular basis to account for changes in your family, your contacts, or the resources in your area. Being ready can make a big difference in making sure your family is safe and healthy during a disaster. You can be a huge asset to the adults in your family by providing your knowledge and experience during an emergency, but remember, they are in charge. Listening to them and offering advice in a respectful way is key.

CONCLUSION

This empowering guide is designed to help you stay safe while adventuring through the wilderness! Remember, like all things in life, practicing skills before you need them is important for mastering them. Ask your friends and family to help you learn the skills in this book long before something goes wrong, so you can stay cool and collected no matter what turn your adventure takes! As you turn the final pages of this book, we hope that the lessons you learned here are only a beginning of your story!

Made in the USA
Monee, IL
06 November 2023

45895786R00083